You, Inc.

You, Inc.

*The Art of
Selling
Yourself*

HARRY BECKWITH
CHRISTINE CLIFFORD BECKWITH

**BUSINESS
PLUS**

NEW YORK   BOSTON

Business Plus
Hachette Book Group
237 Park Avenue
New York, NY 10017
Visit our Web site at www.HachetteBookGroup.com

Business Plus is an imprint of Grand Central Publishing.
The Business Plus name and logo is a trademark of Hachette Book
Group, Inc.

Printed in the United States of America

First Edition: March 2007

10 9 8 7 6 5 4

Library of Congress Cataloging-in-Publication Data

Beckwith, Harry.
  You, Inc. : the art of selling yourself / Harry Beckwith and Christine
Clifford Beckwith. — 1st ed.
      p. cm. — (Warner Business)
  ISBN 978-0-446-57821-9
  1. Communication in marketing. 2. Self-presentation. 3. Advertising
agencies—Marketing. I. Title: Guide to selling yourself. II. Beckwith,
Christine Clifford, 1954– III. Title. IV. Warner business books.
  HF5415.123.B42 2007
  658.85—dc22

                                                      2005037520

Book design and text composition by Giorgetta Bell McRee

To Adrian Stump

ACKNOWLEDGMENTS

Done at last, done at last, thank God Almighty, we are done at last!

We are thankful to so many for the chance to do this, and their help:

Our children—speaking of inspiration—Tim, Harry, Will, Brooks, Cole, and Cooper. You bless us beyond words. We hope this book helps you.

To our extended family, including sister Pam Haros and brother-in-law Nick Haros, brothers Greg and James Meyer, Neda Weldele, stepmother Stephanie Meyer, John, Bette, and Bill Clifford, Alice Beckwith, Jim and Becky Powell, and David and Cindy Beckwith for surrounding us with love and support.

To Cliff Greene and Sue Crolick, who started this train in motion; David Potter, Ron Rebholz, William Clebsch, Clifford Rowe, David Kennedy, and Paul Robinson, Harry's great professors; Stephanie Prem and Cathy and Jim Phillips; and John McPhee, E. B. White, Kurt Vonnegut Jr., and Theodor Geisel.

To Pat Miles, Pat and Kathy Lewis, Margie Sborov, Dr. Buck Brown, Larry Gatlin, Ruth Ann

Marshall, Bill Coore, Arnold Palmer, Bob Brown and Bill Bartels, Dr. Burton Schwartz, Dr. Tae Kim, Dr. Margit L. Bretzke, Gerald McCullagh, and Jack Lindstrom.

Thanks Ty Votaw and Bill Passolt.

This book is inconceivable without the continued talent and patience of the people of Warner Books, who continue to prove that parts of New York are as warm as any town in the South: Rick Wolff, of course, Sharon Krassney for what seems like forever, the splendid duo of Giorgetta Bell McRee and Bernadette Evangeliste, and Jason Pinter and Dan Ambrosio.

Harry is particularly indebted to the woman who demonstrated so vividly the wisdom of doing what makes you uncomfortable. He did not want to go to Portland, Oregon, that day to speak, particularly given the compensation package, which was zero. He went anyway, and the compensation turned out to be enormous. He found what he had been missing all his life: Christine. The rest is personal, and too much to explain here, especially in words that many others would understand. "Beyond fabulous," as Christine would say, to which he replies, "Beyond thanks."

This book is dedicated to our nephew Adrian, with our deepest sorrow and hope that our world will be better because of his sacrifice. If so, our world awaits a treat.

CONTENTS

TWO KEY SKILLS:

LISTENING AND SPEAKING **95**

INTRODUCTION

This book actually began as three books. The first, *How to Make $1 Million in Sales ($3 Million Before Taxes)*, was to have been Christine's first book on sales.

Harry, meanwhile, was hatching two books. The first, *Seat Belts and Twin Airbags*, was intended for our sons and others just entering the Real World, a book that Harry hoped would brace them for the collision.

His second book, code-named *Who Moved My Salad Fork?*, covered manners. He also thought of our sons as he conceived this book, hoping that their manners and thoughtfulness would make lives—theirs and others'—better.

Now those three books have become this one.

This book reflects a lesson from a shared experience. We both speak. After just a few presentations, you realize that although your host has asked you to talk about business, your audience wants more. They want inspiration and more fulfilling lives. Some worry if they can find either, much less both, in the world of Work.

Our experience assures us that they can, and

should. Life flies by; we want the trip to feel wonderful.

In search of answers, we examined many sources. We studied thriving people in many of the businesses we worked with. We came across a special few—those whom psychologist and author (*Passages*) Gail Sheehy once dubbed "people of high well-being"—and sat down and talked with them, to see what we might learn and pass along.

We also examined our own experiences, emphasizing mistakes. As our fellow Minnesotan Bob Dylan once sang, "There's no success like failure." Well, that's well and good. But mistakes, while great teachers, are no fun. We hope this book shares our lessons and spares you the agony that went with them, that two heads are better than one but one book is better than three, and that you enjoy reading it as much as we enjoyed writing and living it.

Sixteen Candles and Shrewd Waitresses: What People Buy

———————————

Living Is Selling

It's easy to dislike selling, or even the very idea of it.

From childhood, you are conditioned to dislike it. In frontier tales of snake oil salesmen, plays like *Death of a Salesman* and *Glengarry Glen Ross*, and movies like *Boiler Room*, the images of salespeople radiate gloom. Selling is dishonest, dehumanizing, and cruel, and only the slick survive.

For a time, some do. But let's skip that momentarily. Let's deal, instead, with an easily overlooked fact:

Living is selling.

Start from childhood, and remember all the sales calls you made. You worked up a sales pitch to get your parents to take you to Disney World, raise your allowance, and extend your curfew. You pitched them on sleepovers, a nicer bike, perhaps your first car. For that matter, you sold them on the accident that "Wasn't really my fault" and on a report card that seemed to suggest some backsliding. And on and on.

Your childhood sales career prepared you for adulthood, when you tried to sell your college on admitting you, an employer on hiring you, and the car dealer on dropping $500 from the sticker price.

You sell your friends on going to your favorite restaurant. A husband and wife sell constantly: What movie shall we go to? Who takes the dog to the vet? Who's going to get the groceries?

And on and on.

The question is not, are you a salesperson? The question is, how might you become more effective?

Just as important, how might you make your life richer?

As it turns out, the answer to each question answers the other.

Life is a sale. And the path to success at both living and selling is the same.

The Heart of Every Transaction

Inexperienced salespeople invariably start their pitches with the price and the product, then talk about the company. Only at the end, and perhaps not even then, do they finally sell themselves.

Experienced salespeople proceed in the opposite direction. They sell themselves and their organization, then discuss the product. At the end—at the very end—they say, "Now, let's talk about how little this costs, considering everything that you will get."

The first thing you sell is yourself.

What You Really Sell

We hear the word "popularity" as adults, and it almost sounds like an artifact extracted from the remains of our old schools. The filmmaker John Hughes felt this, and knew that his adult audiences would, too, when he made his classic movie *Sixteen Candles*.

A familiar tale of adolescence and high school, the film contains a classic moment. The Cute Girl is envisioning her future with her Hunk Boyfriend.

She paints for him her picture of their adult bliss together:

"We're married, and we're like the most popular couple in town."

Audiences laugh. But one day we realize life *is* more like high school than we had dreamed, and that inane observation in Hughes's movie describes our future. Meryl Streep once warned us of this, too. "I thought life would be like college, but it isn't," she said. "Life is like high school."

The actress was lamenting that mastery, which professors seemed to value so much, counts for less in life than she had hoped, while popularity seems to matter far more.

Every high school had its Ardis Peters. Her parents were not affluent. Her face appeared more quirky than pretty. She never tried out for cheerleader, and might not have succeeded if she had. Yet we could not resist her, possessed of a quality everyone loved but few understood or could define.

We only knew we liked her. Looking back, our reason is clear: Ardis had a feeling about life that drew you in. Around her, you shared that feeling.

Your memories may go back even further, to your school's Carla Strand. Even at the age of seven she embraced life, and it embraced her back. Everyone wanted to be part of her life, because she enjoyed it so much, and passed it on.

Meryl Streep, Ardis, and Carla suggest an important lesson. Yes, you sell your skills in this life. You sell what you know and can do. If by using your skills you are able to help enough people, you will become secure and may become rich.

Beyond that, however, the most critical thing you sell is literally yourself: *your being.* People "buy" optimists because they enjoy their company. They "buy" people with integrity because people with integrity do what they say they will. Like Maytag washing machines, people with integrity can be relied upon.

Our education points us toward mastering our craft. But how should we behave, act, and feel? Schools don't teach us that, and many teachers set examples we should ignore.

But Meryl Streep, Ardis, and Carla remind us that we did learn something in high school: Attitude matters. *Attitude sells.*

Develop your skills, sharpen them, and then sharpen them more each day. But never forget that people buy *all* of you.

Success and fulfillment come from developing all of you—starting in the deepest parts.

What People Value

To see what people really value, watch when they put their money where their mouths are—literally.

Watch how they tip.

Repeated studies of restaurant guests show that people do not tip any more for efficient and prompt service than they do for flawed and slow service.

Instead, people tip more when the waitperson makes them feel good. If the person very briefly touches the diner, for example, the diner typically tips more. A warm smile, a "Hello again, Mr. Peters," or any other hint of "I like you" all elicit bigger tips, too.

When *The New Yorker* magazine recently reviewed these findings, one commentator announced that he was disturbed. Why do we refuse to pay more for "service quality," but will pay more for trivial little gestures of apparent friendship?

We pay more for those "trivial gestures" because they are not trivial; they are what we value in a service.

People value—and pay more for—the way you make them feel.

Nothing More Than Feelings

One of the world's largest insurance firms recently interviewed other firms to handle its payroll. After interviewing the three finalist firms, the three members of the selection committee were stumped. They decided on a perfect solution.

They flew to each finalist's headquarters, took a short walk around, and "got a feeling" for each place.

When they walked into the third company's lobby, something immediately somehow "just felt right." They stayed but four minutes, and then headed home.

From the airport back home, they called the third company with the multimillion-dollar good news.

So often, that is the difference. Not superior competence. Not more years of experience. Just something tiny, like the feeling that you give people.

People buy feelings.

FROM KISSING IN CHINA TO *GRACELAND*: PLANNING AND PREPARING

———————

"Keeping the End in Mind"

How did we become authors? someone asked.

"We gave a speech."

Years later, people asked how we became speakers. Each of us gave an equally honest answer:

"We wrote a book."

We didn't set out to become speakers or authors. We simply kept doing what we loved. There was no end in mind. There was only a path that we loved walking.

And that path began with: "Christine, you should be a writer." People asked why I had never pursued my passion. I always gave the same answer: I couldn't think of a subject I knew enough about.

Four weeks after my surgery for breast cancer in December 1994, I woke in the middle of the night with a vision: cartoons. Almost fifty cancer-related cartoons started filling my head.

Days, weeks, months passed by as I trudged on through my treatments. My cartoons became a focus as I searched for signs of humor in my predicament. The harder I looked, the more I found.

Twelve months later I signed a contract for not

one, but two books on using humor to cope with cancer, filled with those cartoons. Had I set a "goal" of becoming an author, I might never have written a book. I just kept following my passions and one night, two books popped up.

As a 1970s era Nike poster put it so well, "There is no finish line." There is no "end." Life goes until it stops. You head for some paradise, then realize it isn't. Or you arrive at your destination only to realize it isn't the end. Often, it's not even a stop along the way.

Should you set goals? Perhaps, particularly if you need them to stir you to action. But if only goals stir you to action, set another goal:

Find your motivation in something other than goals.

Where should you look? Deeper.

The Real Role of Goal-Setting

In his early years and near poverty, actor Jim Carrey wrote a note on a piece of paper, stuck it in his shirt pocket, and kept it there until he no longer needed it.

The note read, "Make a million dollars."

From stories like Jim Carrey's, we assume that setting goals is the first step to achieving them. We assume Jim Carrey made a million dollars because he set it as a goal and wrote it down. It's a rare self-improvement book, we suspect, that does not stress, "Set goals."

But we misunderstand goal-setting.

First, you have set goals even if you've never written them down. You want to watch what you eat, run three miles with less effort, get closer to your father. You rarely think about these "goals." But at one time, those thoughts crossed your mind, and you devoted yourself to them. You set goals; few human beings do not.

But the value of goal-setting does not come just from the goals. It comes from the thinking that went into the planning, and the knowledge that comes out. Set goals with others and you learn. You learn what others value, and learn more about them, and that helps you make better and more informed decisions every day.

In business, the same regularly proves itself. The value of a business plan rarely comes from the goals and strategies. Those goals and strategies change so early and often that most business plans are better viewed as, "What do we plan to do until we change our minds?" That we ignore these plans does not matter. What matters is what happened as you made the plan:

Everyone learned.

Set goals not because they will help you reach them, but because they will teach you.

So Who Are You?

To steal one of the ancient slogans in advertising, your brand is the truth about you, well told.

Like every company, every person has a dozen good stories that reveal that person. A talent in marketing is to discover your stories—some the enterprise has forgotten, ignored, or overlooked—and tell them well.

That's your task, too. *What is your story—the true story?*

How can you tell it best?

You may need help. An outsider or someone who knows you well can give you perspective.

Start there. Get help, if necessary, but do it:

Find your story, tell it well.

What Do You Do?

Most venture capitalists, who make some of the largest purchases in all of sales, ask two questions of companies that come to them for money and help.

Their first question is simple, but the answers often are not:

What do you—or whatever you are selling—do?

You must answer simply, too. Otherwise you will confuse the person. If it sounds like you do many things, or too many seemingly unrelated things, the person will assume you cannot do any of them well.

Ask that question. Write down your answer. Show it to four people whose opinion you value. Ask them:

Is it clear?

Is it simple?

Does it inspire their confidence that you are focused enough to master whatever you are selling?

Ask and answer: What do you do?

Jack of a Dozen Trades

The speaking industry features hundreds of characters, but eventually you run into a dozen Jacks.

Ask Jack his specialty. Team-building? Change? Creativity and Innovation? Leadership? Sales?

Yes, he answers; all five! Plus Motivation, Marketing, and four other topics.

You might wonder if you are talking to a modern Erasmus, the last man reputed to know everything. You puzzle, too, because Jack appears to be about forty. Yet in just eighteen years of business, he apparently has become expert at virtually everything except Finance and IT.

What would you hire Jack to do, knowing how many things he apparently can do?

Nothing.

You will never recall Jack's specialty, or ever think of him if the subject of Leadership arises, because Jack has overwhelmed your memory with a list of skills so long you cannot recall any one of them.

Worse, and obviously, he clearly has marked himself not as an expert on several subjects, but as an expert on none.

People know that Jacks of All Trades are Masters of None, and people seek out masters. They trust specialists. Try to appeal to thousands, and you will appeal strongly to no one.

Find a niche. Even if you range widely, find out what your inquirer needs and focus your message on that need only.

Ask: What is your specialty? (And have one.)

What Difference
Do You Make?

The second question to ask yourself, after asking "What do you do?" seems logical, yet challenging. It is a challenge to which you must rise:

"Why does it matter?"

What difference do you—or what you are selling—make?

Marketers often refer to the necessity of defining one's "point of difference." This language is significant. You must not merely answer what makes you different, but how what you do makes a difference for others.

Ask that question. Write down that answer. Show it to four people whose opinion you value.

Demand they be ruthlessly tough with their answers.

Ask and answer: What is the difference you, or what you are selling, make?

Your Third Question

Part of the genius of Southwest Airlines is that their leader, Herb Kelleher, constantly asks his employees a third question:

Are we a company that our competitors envy?

If not, why not?

Apply that to whatever you are selling and then to yourself.

Ask, "If not, why not? And what can I do to change that?"

Are you enviable? How can you make yourself enviable?

Question Four, and the Power of Stereotypes

We presented a breakthrough advertising campaign for the manufacturer of large monitors for

Apple computers. We even offered an unexpected added value: an ingenious new name for the company and their monitor—"tattoos for the brain," as some call the powerful brand names.

The client was dazzled, and told us. Loved the strategy, the creative, the advertisements, the copy, even our shoes and ties.

We drove home from the presentation and called Haskell's Wine & Spirits for two bottles of champagne.

We waited for the good news. It never came. They awarded the business to BBD&O.

Finally we called, perplexed. But you loved our work, said it was the best.

"It was. The most strategic and most creative work we saw."

"Then why didn't you choose us?"

"Well, it's just that Harry is a lawyer. *And lawyers can't be creative.*"

People don't think; they stereotype. They don't conclude; they categorize. They don't calculate; they assume.

As evidence, look at this list and free-associate, noting your first response to each word:

> Volvo driver
> Goatee
> Texan

Face-lift
Catholic priest

What just happened?

Don't worry. We *all* do it. But do you see how automatically and subconsciously we do it?

Everyone stereotypes. The esteemed psychologist William James expressed it perfectly: "The first thing an intellect does with an object is to classify it along with something else."

It's easy to see why we do this. For convenience and survival, our brains evolved to organize data according to apparent patterns. We learn to associate black with death and formality, for example. We stereotype—instantly.

It's not thinking, but an easier substitute. You cannot really study someone in an effort to understand them without working hard. Most of us never submit to that ordeal, partly because we aren't certain that we will reach the right conclusion even after careful study.

Our stereotypes aren't accurate, but they help. Our time, after all, is short.

That's why Americans immediately ask a new acquaintance, "So what do you do for a living?" The answer lets us categorize the person. Accountant? Stiff. Lawyer? Arrogant. Engineer? Analytical. Author? Nonconformist. Our mind paints a quick picture—paint that obscures our view of the unique person behind it.

Shown tapes of a "Statistics Professor" and another of a "Humanistic Psychology Professor," one group of Nalini Ambady's Harvard students found the first man "cold, remote, and tense," while the second group found the "humanist" "warm and deeply concerned with students." *They were the same man.*

In advising companies, a good marketer never merely asks, "What is your current position in your market?" It's a vital question. But it's not the only vital question to ask immediately.

The second key question is, "How are companies in your industry, and the people in them, perceived?"

What's the stereotype?

Ask this of yourself, too.

Before you try to make any sale, ask: How is this person likely to stereotype me?

What to Look For

What situations in business make you uncomfortable?

Write them down.

What is your feeling?

Where did it start, and how long ago?

Who can you talk to about this, and get you past it?

The situations that make you uncomfortable in business are those when you are at your weakest and most vulnerable. At these moments you make your biggest mistakes, the ones that are inhibiting you from performing and feeling better.

Attack these and your life will accelerate.

This isn't the easiest advice to hear, and among the hardest to follow. But it's precisely for both of those reasons that hearing and following this will lead you to someplace special. Because most people, hearing this, turn the other way, repeat their mistakes, suffer in silence, and hold themselves back.

Don't. Every week, do this exercise. Like heavy weight work, it will leave you sore. Do it each week, however, and it will make you stronger.

When you reach a point where you've gone as

far as you can, find someone to push you the rest of the way—the equivalent of the workout partner upon whom most athletes rely to maximize their growth.

To truly thrive, learn what makes you uncomfortable.

Work the Weakness

Visit a golf driving range some afternoon and you see human nature hard at work.

You see a dozen people hitting much better shots, on average, than they hit on a golf course. Each will tell you that if he struck the ball this well on the golf course, he'd shrink his handicap seven shots.

They also think they have the explanation. They feel more relaxed hitting balls when nothing is at stake. Put a green in front of them and a scorecard in their pocket, however, and their knuckles turn white, and the ball flies everywhere but straight ahead.

Their tension and anxiety explain a few bad shots per round. The explanation for those other seven or eight shots, however, is simple. Indeed, it's right in the golfer's hand:

They are practicing shots with their favorite club.

If a golfer hits her seven-iron better than any other club, that is precisely the club she is holding. (Except when it's her driver, because every golfer wants to hit longer drives.)

As in golf, so in the rest of our lives. We practice our strengths but ignore our weaknesses.

You can see the waste. You can only improve your strengths so much, if at all. Even if you improve them, there's a good chance no one will notice; slight improvements are hard to spot. What people do notice are your weaknesses; if you can improve those, your improvement can be dramatic, and visible to everyone.

Find your weaknesses and work on them.

Be grateful for your strengths, but work on your weaknesses.

Jumping to
Conclusions

The solution appeared obvious to the firm's creative people.

Their client operated in a female-dominated business (61 percent) whose prospects were predominantly female, too (63 percent): veterinary medicine.

Having learned that women dominate both sides of the table—the doctor and the pet owner— the agency decided that whatever name they recommended should appeal strongly to women.

The creatives brainstormed several hundred names and winnowed them down to a final list of twelve. Then the researchers tested them, formally and informally, to see the reaction.

The more feminine the name, the more negative the response—*from women!* Men actually responded better, but not positively.

Pink, purple, anything with flowers: women hated those names. But of course, the agency people thought: women hate pink, purple, and flowers. But wait, they don't.

Just as you might have assumed that this service involved fashion, perfume, or cosmetics, they assumed something, too. They assumed wrong.

We leap to conclusions as quickly as we rush to judgments. We feel confident in our assumptions, but so often learn we are wrong.

Fortunately, the firm had created fail-safes against its assumptions. It relied on others—panels and groups—for complete perspectives on how people think, and how they react to specific words.

You may be less protected from these errors, but only if you choose to be. You can reach out to others, too, and you should. Seek second, third, and fourth opinions.

Don't assume; *ask*. Does this sentence work? Ask six people.

Does this make sense? Ask six more.

Should I wear this to the meeting with the subcontractor? Ask.

You will gain strength from these numbers. The more people who can shed light on your challenges, the better your chances of overcoming them.

People can challenge your assumptions, and by doing that, lead you to better decisions.

Don't assume. Ask.

Mentor—Or Mentors?

Conventional wisdom once said that you needed a mentor.

This conclusion, however, proved to be based on a typical mistake. The sources of this wisdom confused a coincidence with a cause.

No doubt many successful people have had mentors. (Many did not, something these discussions always overlook.) But knowing that successful people had mentors does not prove the person succeeded because of their mentors. For all we know, they might have succeeded in spite of them.

The reason that many successful people had mentors is that people destined to succeed attract all kinds of people, including mentors. They attract mentors, fans, followers, even puppies and kittens.

So the way to attract a mentor is to display those traits that will lead you to success anyway. Will a mentor lead you there? Probably not. Will one help you in some smaller way? Probably.

Don't seek a mentor. Instead, focus on doing the things that might attract people, including mentors.

If you do find a mentor, make sure you have others. Mentors are people, people are fallible, and even gifted doctors misdiagnose. Fortunately in many of those cases, the patient sought second and third opinions.

You should, too.

Having a mentor is overrated; having several is not.

The Key to Success

Many experts on architecture, as well as its fans, consider Frank Lloyd Wright the world's greatest modern architect. Yet he struggled.

The figure of myth Icarus was brilliant, too. He could fashion wings, glue them with wax, and fly to the heavens. Like Wright, Icarus lacked humility. Thinking he could fly among the gods, he flew too near the sun, and perished when the sun melted his wings.

General George Patton was brilliant, too—as he

was too fond of reminding anyone who suggested there might be another way to win World War II.

You find people like this everywhere, and it prompts this question: Are strengths the key to your success?

Only in part. Your strengths will take you only as far as your weaknesses will allow.

Everywhere you see people who could be so successful, and then you add the two magic words:

If only.

If only he would listen better. If only he could control his temper. If only he did not play politics. If only he would fix his teeth, or that bad habit of . . .

If only.

A bold and successful boss—for his modesty's sake, we call him Andrew—helped forge a uniquely successful firm because he was a master of confronting *If Only.* Annually, and in some years more often, he would hire another Future Star from among hundreds of dazzling applicants. Being merely human, each applicant suffered from an *If Only.* Fortunately, these talented young men and women had something else.

They had Andrew.

Andrew combined personal courage and a conviction that his role was to make sure Future Stars became Stars, with his company or without it. Before the *If Only* became career-limiting, Andrew would summon the Star to his office.

You are destined for great things, but must work on this, he'd tell them. This summit meeting became known as the Annual Visit.

Andrew is special. He is among those rare men who can answer the inevitable wife's question, "Does this dress make me look fat?", with an answer that is honest, well received, and helpful.

Everyone needs an Andrew.

Find your Andrew.

Seek Tough Love

It's comforting to hear you are doing great.

It doesn't help you, however.

"Don't you just love these effects you can generate with PowerPoint?" you ask a colleague. Could she ever answer "No"?

Never. It's human nature.

It's tempting to seek praise, but better to plea for criticism. You will only receive it, however, if you know how to ask. Fortunately, the experience of marketers can help you.

Marketers have discovered the same problem. Despite what you may think, and despite how often you are frustrated with the service you receive, you almost never complain to the company. As a result, virtually everyone in every company assumes they are serving people well, just as you do, because they hear so few complaints.

Complaints will not come voluntarily.

You will not receive these "constructive criticisms" if you ask someone, as businesses conducting surveys often do, "What are we doing wrong?"

That question invites harsh criticism. Because most people hate to be criticized, and are pained by it, they resist answering.

Human beings, however, readily offer advice; many offer it without being asked and most are flattered when they are asked. But how do you get them to offer advice?

Don't ask, "What am I doing wrong?"

Ask, "What could I do to be even more effective?"

As a variation of this, phrase your question, "I

think this might work, but I value your opinion. What might work even better?"

To get the right help, ask the right questions.

Cultivating an Image

In a well-known commercial, tennis player Andre Agassi once proffered the advice that "Image is everything."

That same year, a prospective client asked us to help him cultivate an image. We posed a positioning question to him: "What makes you unique in your business?"

He answered, "Class. I'm classy."

The comment sounded self-liquidating. Would a "classy" person say that?

He wanted us to help him cultivate an image.

You can't.

The person behind your veneer comes through eventually, if not immediately. Once it does, people no longer will know you for your image or your essence. They will know you as someone who tries to fool them.

It's been tried many times.

Interestingly enough, Agassi realized the folly in his words. Within years he had shaved off his mullet hair, abandoned his Day-Glo clothes, and settled into spousehood with a woman whose un-made-up face and entire manner suggested someone with no interest in image, Steffi Graf. He devoted himself to charity and humility, suddenly as open to the world as the top of his now bald head.

Did our prospective client undergo a similar transformation? It appeared so. Two years ago we collided in a health club. His old lacquered veneer seemed gone. You felt you were hearing him and not just well-chosen words aimed for effect. He seemed to have found humility. But he was forty-five now; he'd waited a little long, and his trail of professional nonsuccesses was among the prices he had paid.

Project yourself.

People Decide, Then Think

People rarely make decisions as a product of long deliberation. They may take weeks to announce a decision but often make the decision in minutes, even seconds. People do not gather data to make a decision; they often gather it to *justify* their decision. They are not accumulating understanding; they are seeking comfort and support.

Most decisions are made, then justified, rather than the other way around.

One obvious implication: "First impressions are lasting" understates the actual case. The first impression, with startling frequency, is also the final decision.

The first thing to plan for is your first impression.

People Buy You
with Their Eyes

Time and again in sales and marketing, we realize a powerful influence: *The visual overwhelms the verbal.* In expressing this to clients, we often use the phrases "People think with their eyes" and "People hear what they see."

A vivid example: a presentation of a commercial to a group of small business owners. The commercial stressed three times the bank's point of difference: the bank had the information people needed to make better financial decisions. To illustrate how people use information to make good decisions, the commercial showed an Everest climber preparing—studying maps and weather charts—before making his ascent. But the viewers of the commercial didn't hear the "information" words at all, despite the fact that the copy repeated those words three times in thirty seconds.

When asked what the commercial was saying, the viewers responded, "It was about strength. The bank is communicating that it is strong."

The commercial's creators were stunned. Not only did they not intend to communicate "strong."

They were not aware that they could have.

Where did the viewers get that idea? From one image that flashed on-screen for less than four seconds: a shot of the man rock-climbing.

One picture, three seconds: the visual overwhelmed the verbal.

We think with our eyes.

Watch your visuals carefully.

Your Package

To many people, his ideas sounded obnoxious.

The man was John Molloy, and his ideas were expressed in a book whose title became part of the American vocabulary: *Dress for Success*.

Many rebelled at the very thought of it. Dressing for Success sounded manipulative—the cousin of ideas like those of Michael Korda, who advised executives to make sure their office chairs stood taller than the others, so they would appear superior.

But Molloy was not advising manipulation, any more than the advice birds might give to other birds, whose appearances often make them targets for attacks from other birds. Odd plumage has that effect—on birds and people.

Molloy was not counseling cleverness and manipulation. He was reflecting his conviction that success in life, like simple manners, begins with a mindfulness of others and a sensitivity to our impact on them. Molloy was not counseling men to wear massive gold watches so that others would assume them rich. More often, he advised the opposite: Understate, don't overstate.

Many people who know this still rebel at the thought of dressing mindfully. "I want to be me," or "I do as I please," and, very often, "I don't want to deal with people who are influenced by things like dress and appearance."

Review those words. What do they clearly imply? You come first. Do you want to work with that person? Do you want that person as an employee, a service provider, or a friend?

America at the time was entering the Age of Narcissism, as one sage named it. The slogan "Looking out for number one" had achieved bumper sticker and T-shirt status. In that milieu, it was easy to deride Molloy as another advocate of self-absorption and self-worship. But Molloy was not suggesting that you look inside. He was saying look *outside*.

What is your impact on others? Are you sabotaging yourself without knowing it? Are you losing the battle before the shooting even begins?

Molloy was essentially speaking from the spirit that informs good manners. He was saying, "Be mindful."

Being mindful begins when you open your closet.

Visuals and Stereotyping

Most movie fans agree that the ending of *The Usual Suspects* ranks among the greatest in movie history.

Like so many great endings, this one startles you.

The ending depends on a classic example of misdirection. The architect of this trick play—a trick on both his police interrogator and the viewer—is played by actor Kevin Spacey. Spacey plays the role of a slow-witted cripple. He has been implicated in a theft, explosion, and multiple murder involving four con men—confident, strong, and clever men who are nothing like Spacey, the odd duck in this fivesome.

Near the movie's end Spacey, apparently because of his limited intelligence and a team of clever interrogators, foolishly reveals the details of the crime.

Spacey discloses that a Keyser Söze masterminded the crime. Spacey goes into tiny details, right down to hearing a barbershop quartet in Skokie, Illinois. After hearing these minute details, the interrogator offers Spacey protection from Söze, who is hunting Spacey down, if he will retell the story in court. Spacey refuses, insists that he is not a rat, and eventually limps out of the room and on to the street.

The interrogator, played by Chazz Palminteri, contemplates the story that he has unraveled.

Then *it* unravels.

Palminteri scans his office billboard behind him, which Spacey faced throughout their discussion. He notices the word "Quartet," the name of the billboard's manufacturer, at the bottom of the board's frame. Palminteri scans down from that word and sees two more words right below.

"Skokie, Illinois."

In a rush, Palminteri sees a dozen other words on the billboard and realizes Spacey has fabricated his entire story from those words. Spacey has conned him.

The camera cuts to the outside and a closeup of Spacey's limp, which quickly disappears and is replaced with a confident stride. Spacey enters a getaway car and flees.

The viewer and the interrogator become convinced that Spacey is a mere dupe in this massive scheme not just because of his manner, but the power of a vivid visual: Spacey's pronounced limp. We decide Spacey must be intellectually and emotionally weak because he is crippled physically. We fall into that stereotype so easily we never realize it happened, nor question afterward our stereotypes about disabled people: the belief that one disability gives evidence of others.

The reverse is true, too, of course, which is why we choose visual clues—serious suits, serious briefcases—that make us appear competent. As *The Usual Suspects* reminds us, visual clues work. They even can convince an experienced detective that a cunning man is a dimwit.

Watch your visual clues, to trigger the right stereotypes.

Packaging Against Your Stereotype

The first obstacle you must overcome is not your competition; it's the stereotype outsiders have of you.

Before you present yourself, whatever your purpose, ask yourself the day before, "What do they know about me?

"What impressions have they already formed from what little they already know?"

Then ask, "Does my appearance reinforce their stereotype?"

If so, package yourself to undermine the stereotype. An artist in a well-tailored suit, a U.S. President in a cardigan sweater (one tried that), an engineer with a tattoo; these are not necessarily the best answers in a particular situation, but examples of ways to attack a stereotype.

A uniquely successful advertising creative director succeeded not simply because he created good ideas for clients, but because he starred at selling them. After several months, we noticed a trick he used that he confessed seemed to work.

"If our campaign appears conservative, I dress more creatively, to give the impression that we can go to the edge but deliberately chose not to." He followed the opposite strategy when his group developed a risky approach: he wore his darkest suit, black lace-up shoes, and the tie you'd choose when you go to your bank for a loan.

One benefit that many professionals reaped from Casual Fridays, and the spread of them throughout their workweek, is that many new clients began to perceive these professionals as more relaxed and accessible.

Yet another professional firm, an advertising agency, benefited from a different approach. They dressed up only on Fridays. "We're not casual here at all," they said. "We only dress that way Monday through Thursday for the same reason construction workers do. We work hard."

To defeat a stereotype, dress contrary to it.

Investing in You

If you ask an advisor to small businesses, "What is the biggest mistake you see them make?," you will get an important answer.

On their list of the top three mistakes, and often at the top, is a dismaying one:

"They didn't invest enough."

As a result, their execution looked half-baked. They looked tentative, as if they feared their idea was flawed and lacked the faith to put their money behind it.

Like businesses of many, this lesson applies powerfully to the Business of One. Consider this powerful example from Christine:

In 1997, Schering Oncology/Biotech purchased over 50,000 copies of our Cancer Club exercise video, designed for women recovering from breast cancer.

With this success, we realized that Bristol-Myers Squibb represented another great prospect. They had retained Lance Armstrong as their spokesperson, and I already had spoken at several Bristol-sponsored events.

I contacted Bristol's local sales representative, who in turn referred me to their district manager.

Three weeks later, great news: the district manager was intrigued by our offer and had forwarded the information to Corporate.

Rebecca at Corporate was intrigued, too. So intrigued that she called to say, "Come to New Jersey. I want you to meet our entire Marketing Department. I think we should do business."

That sounded like, "You have won the Powerball."

Ten days later, I landed at Newark Airport. Being frugal and realizing the trip was entirely at my expense, I decided to rent a car.

Then the troubles began.

My suitcases were so heavy with Cancer Club products that it took me what seemed like an eternity to hoist them off the baggage claim and onto my carrier. Because my suitcases were so large, I could not take them on an escalator up to the car rental facility. I had to take the elevator.

Unfortunately, only one elevator went to the car rental facility, and it was having an off day. I ended up having to haul the bags up the stairs instead, and . . .

Wait. You get the picture—except for the part that I was so anxious by the time I finally got everything into my car that I left the airport and for fifteen minutes headed—in the opposite direction from Princeton.

I arrived at Bristol's compound, looking as if I'd just finished a 10K. Here at last, until I looked at the four large buildings in front of me. Which was Rebecca's? My map didn't say.

I headed to Building One. When I arrived there, the receptionist said I wanted Building Four.

I called Rebecca to explain my plight. I got her voice mail.

When I finally got to Building Four, the receptionist there handed me the phone. It was Rebecca. When I didn't appear, she and her marketing team ate their lunch and waited until they could wait no longer; they had other meetings.

End of opportunity. No one wants to risk working with someone who appears seventy-five minutes late for a meeting. If I had booked a car service, it would have delivered me to Princeton ten minutes before the meeting. Instead, I chose to save $115, and lost a $125,000 opportunity in the process.

You have to invest. The investments you make, of both time and money, demonstrate your confidence in what you are offering. The premium prices you pay are literally that: premiums. They are your insurance in your success.

I overlooked that once. I never have again.

Pay more now, reap more later.

Tricks and Shortcuts

There are none.

Thinking Outside
Your Box

"We need to think outside the box."

No, you don't.

It's a lyric heard every minute, somewhere in the world. But the message doesn't work.

Here's why, and what you should do instead.

Your box—your way of thinking, working, and living—has worked for you. It's the box in which you were born, a product of the DNA with which you were encoded. You can change your box about as easily as you can alter the shape of your head.

You are methodical or mercurial; you are lateral

or linear; you tend to be inward, or outward. But from birth, you are who you are. It's a pretty good box. Most important, it is yours—the box in which you have operated forever.

Don't try to think outside your box; it's too hard. Instead, grow it.

For a wonderful inspiration and example, consider the story of the singer Paul Simon.

Simon wrote some of our previous century's classic songs, including an album that became the background music for an entire generation: *Bookends*. Millions bought it, and millions more heard its songs as the background music to the movie classic *The Graduate*.

Simon flourished inside his box. His box was filled with the culture of rebellious 1960s America, torn between chasing California girls on the beach on one hand and protesting the Vietnam War on the other.

Simon flourished inside his box—and then he didn't. He stayed there, and the box that had helped him produce classics started producing fluff like "Kodachrome." ("He should be arrested for that song," a recovering Simon fan once said.) Simon's box closed in on him.

Simon solved it, but not by changing his thinking. He changed his box by bringing new things into it. To find them he ventured a world away; he flew to

Africa. There, his box changed from what he felt and saw. As he wrote in one song, he saw "angels in the architecture, spinning in infinity."

Africa and its images and sounds startled, moved, and overwhelmed Simon. With his head stirring with these new influences, and inspired by the African group Ladysmith Black Mambazo, he wrote "You Can Call Me Al" and one of music's truly outside-the-box creations, the album *Graceland*.

Simon didn't think outside his box; few people can. Simon grew his box. He brought into it new things, studied different cultures, and listened to African music rather than his own.

From that he transformed himself, and flourished.

To become more creative—always a good idea—don't try to think outside your box. Instead, grow it. Bring new things in.

If you read *Vanity Fair*, read *In-Fisherman*. If you read *Tattoo*, pick up an *Architectural Digest*. If you read *People*, scan *The New Yorker*. If you attend the theater, catch a NASCAR race (not least of all, because of its immense appeal). If you'd never dream of watching ballet, listening to bluegrass, or going to a county fair, *go*.

Tinker with your box. Buy an orange sport coat and a pair of red suede shoes; see what changes.

Grow a bigger box.

Education's Overlooked Rewards

Anyone who observes high school juniors and seniors recognizes a widely held view about education: we educate ourselves to prepare for our careers.

With some exceptions, this point of view morphs into the view that classes must be "relevant," and that if we are preparing for a career in business, we should major in it. Failing that, we should take "practical" courses.

But we see education too narrowly and cheat ourselves of one of its rewards.

To illustrate this myopia, consider the high school senior who decides to major in business. "Why learn about American history, civil engineering, or agronomy?" he might reasonably ask.

He chooses not to learn anything about these subjects. Then he ventures into the Real World. During just one twelve-month period, he meets a history buff (the South, thanks to the Civil War, teems with them), a civil engineer, and the greenskeeper for a local golf course.

How does the young man engage these three people? By finding common ground. If he has even a glimpse of knowledge—a recollection of Antietam or Lee's blunder at Gettysburg, the role of nitrous oxide in Atlanta air pollution, or an understanding of why the greenest lawns actually are among the least healthy—he can strike a conversation, and then a chord.

If all he can talk about is the narrow sphere in which he operates, he will continue to be confined to that sphere.

Education does more than prepare us for careers and expand our minds. It enlarges our world—the number of people with whom we can connect. Because education covers so much ground, it helps us find more of the ground that is common to others whom we meet.

The more you learn, the more people you can engage. All education is relevant, all education is practical, all education helps us grow.

Keep reading, keep listening, keep learning.

Taking This Book
to Santiago

Six thousand seven hundred miles south of Los Angeles, in a spot closer to the South Pole than to North America, you come upon the beautiful Chilean capital city of Santiago.

A curious visitor, intrigued by how this city may be different from those back home, might venture to the largest shopping center and learn a remarkable lesson.

He *is* home. There it is: Revlon, Tommy Hilfiger, L'Oréal, Orange Julius. Where are the Chilean products? Where is the Abercrombie & Fitch of South America? It's nowhere.

So travelers today experience something odd. They can visit a dozen countries and never leave the same mall.

Venture into Beijing's Forbidden City, hallowed by the Chinese for centuries, and you will eventually turn a corner and feel your breath taken away. There, deep in the center of this sacred place, is a monument:

Starbucks.

Granted, you find differences in cultures. Islam still influences even the most Westernized Muslim women and men in India. Dine with a few who drive German cars and wear Italian suits, and you will notice the influence: no one orders meat or alcohol. But look at the copy of *The Hindustan* newspaper, and you will feel at home. The dominant news item commands not just the front page, but the Business, Style, Entertainment, and Sports sections. The news is of the "Big Game." (It's cricket, India versus Pakistan.)

Sports in the Style and Entertainment sections? Of course! What are people wearing to matches? More importantly, who do India's top directors and leading actors and actresses think will win? Who do people consider the sexiest player on each team? To show how "American" India can seem, people there have coined a shorthand for its world of movies and the area in Bombay where most Indian movies are made:

They call it Bollywood.

People seem remarkably similar, wherever we travel. In *Human Universals*, Donald Brown listed the human traits that he had discovered in every culture. His list required forty-four pages and included over 250 shared traits, including singing, dancing, joke-telling, sexual modesty, revenge-seeking, etiquette, a preference for faces with "average" features, even the fear of snakes.

Does this book apply wherever you go? It does.

Yes, be aware of local differences. When you first greet a woman in Chile, for example, you immediately should give her a kiss on each cheek. Otherwise you risk offending her. Try this in China, however, and you will find yourself kissing air and then pulling back to notice a startled-looking woman. Her face tells you she had no idea what you intended, and prays you never try that again.

But while gestures and nuances change, the desires and demands are universal. We want to be appreciated and respected, and we reciprocate when we are.

Apply these lessons everywhere.

Hogs, Apples, and Writer's Underwear: Communicating

How to Play the Shift

For several thousand years, people conducted life and business face-to-face.

That phrase "face-to-face" is significant here. We once dealt with others not just personally, but in person; we worked in offices where we saw each other hourly and met at least weekly. Outside, clients tended to be within walking distance or driving distance, and we jumped on planes for those who were farther away. We transacted even distant business by phone, where our presence mattered: an authoritative voice, by definition, conveys and reinforces authority.

Physical presence mattered immensely then. The power to make a powerful visual impression mattered so much, in fact, that a study showed that every inch of a man's height was worth almost a thousand dollars a year in salary.

Presence still matters, but a shift has occurred.

Today, e-mail, airplanes, and globalization have caused a shift. More of our communications are written, sent across hundreds of miles. As a result, the authoritative written voice has started to replace the importance of the authoritative physical presence.

Ask human resource directors and major corporate executives what skill matters most in today's business. They answer, "The ability to communicate."

The face-to-face meeting allowed us to act and interact, question and answer. At the end of the meeting, the parties typically achieved something approaching clarity. With e-mail, clarity becomes more important as time has become more valuable—not least of all because staffs have shrunk.

Ambiguity is expensive; it forces us to go back and forth, often several times, to clarify our meaning and move to the next step. As a result, the ambiguous communicator represents an expense.

More and more, power comes from the words of the communicator, and the most potent words are those that are expressed succinctly and vividly. Those who can express themselves in words that cannot be misunderstood have more power, and more value.

And so we see a perceptible shift from the Power Tie and the Power Breakfast. Indeed, it's a sign of the shift that those terms appear to have disappeared. Increasingly, we live in the age of the Power Note, Power Memo, and Power Proposal.

The future belongs to the Communicators.

Selling to the Overwhelmed

You are trying to sell yourself to people who feel overwhelmed.

To appreciate this, try to buy toothpaste, for example. If you've decided you want to switch from the one you are using, how can you hope to find a replacement? In the typical Target store, you confront rows of over sixty options, including pastes with whitener, tartar control, breath-freshening, baking powder, tube and pump, in over a dozen different brands. In developing countries, researchers have learned that this sheer number of products ranks among the five greatest concerns of the people.

We *feel* overwhelmed. Our DVD players have more functions than we can learn. When something goes wrong, few of us know what to do.

We *are* overwhelmed. Everyone you deal with is overwhelmed. Whatever you want to communicate to them, you must learn to do it simply.

Simplify and clarify.

The *Real* First Rule
of Communicating

An important government document once cost the country over $100 million because the writer used a semicolon rather than a comma.

That document seemed clear enough to the writer—just as all of our communications do. None of us ever sends a document we think may be unclear. Yet every day, we receive documents that are.

When we communicate, we assume that the first rule is, "Communicate so that you are understood." It's not.

The first rule is: *Communicate so that you cannot be misunderstood.*

In analyzing extraordinary business relationships, you soon learn that clarity places high on the list—among the most significant eight or nine key influences.

Clarity inspires trust. We worry about the opposite: we fear that people we do not understand may be concealing something. We suspect the confusion might be a smoke screen, intended to keep us from the truth.

Clarity inspires faith. We assume—as jurors assume when they hear expert witnesses—that a person who communicates clearly understands his subject. A leading jury-consulting firm, in fact, has found that people regard "clarity" as the signal trait of a true expert—even more significant than a reputed expert's professional accomplishments and awards.

Make yourself clearer, and people will think you are an expert.

Simplify

What we want most is certainty; we find ways to deal with certainty. What we can't deal with is the opposite. A popular expression captures this feeling perfectly:

"I was paralyzed with doubt."

You approach someone with a proposition: you want a job, an audience, a reference—something. You outline your proposition at length, covering every angle, making an overwhelming case.

That was the problem. Your case *was* overwhelming. The listener felt overwhelmed.

You went too far.

The detailed, point-by-point elaboration squelches everything. You provide so much detail, and now the listener feels perplexed. Your proposition is complicated. Because we speak and hear imperfectly, your excessive detail actually has confused your listener; some parts seem contradictory. And there are *so* many options.

(In marketing, we refer to this as option paralysis. The phenomenon appeared most vividly in tests in which shoppers were given the choice of three different types of strawberry jam. They choose one. When given four additional choices, however, they walked away empty-handed.)

Make it simple. Constantly edit your story.

You cannot say too little in such a situation. For one thing, if you advance one strong argument, you will get your listener's attention and she will ask for more. Her specific questions will tell you what she wants to know, and spare you the wasted effort of discussing anything else—and confusing the listener more.

Simplify. Simplicity gives people certainty, and certainty they can deal with.

What Wal-Mart Tells You

Until a few months ago, the clothing racks in Wal-Mart stores stood one inch shorter than Shaquille O'Neal. Today, they stand just four feet six inches.

Wal-Mart's change reveals something that people want: space.

The old Wal-Mart overwhelmed people with stacks and racks of merchandise.

Today, shoppers can see over each rack, and in most stores they can remove the merchandise from the racks without a hard yank.

Wal-Mart has learned that less is more.

Speakers know this. They focus not just on words, but on silence. As in great music, the pauses matter, too; a pause gives the listener and musician a chance to breathe. It causes you to anticipate what might come next, and to appreciate what came before.

Advertisers know this. Perhaps the greatest ads of our era, for the Apple iPod, are filled not with words, but with white space. (Or, to be technically accurate, chartreuse or blue space, the dominant colors in the iPod palette.) A black silhouette of someone dancing, a white silhouette of an iPod in the dancer's chest, and three words: "Life is random."

Decades ago, Rudolph Flesch discovered that readers were not just attracted to words, but to the breathing room between sentences and paragraphs. Long sentences should be followed by short ones, and large paragraphs should be followed by short ones, he decided.

Follow Flesch's prescription. Try to reduce your average sentences to eleven words. If you must write a large block of copy, try to place a short one in front of it and behind it.

While speaking, practice your pauses. If making an important point, precede it with a pregnant pause, which alerts your listener: "This is important."

Then follow it with a pause, so that your point has time to take root.

Watch your white space. Silence talks.

The Writer's Underwear

In writing, some call it "the writer's underwear."

Everywhere you look, it's flashing in the breeze.

It's there when a speaker talks about "consulting with HP in Rome."

Or when the graphic designer adds some flourishes to a logo that all but shout, "Look how clever I am."

Or when someone chooses an erudite-sounding word when a simpler one would communicate better.

In each case, the communicator has misunderstood what "to communicate" really means. The word "communicate" and the word "commune" share the same derivation. Each implies a sense of equality: people sharing with one another.

The three examples above do not represent attempts to share something with another for their common benefit. Each communicator is not trying to give anything other than an impression: I am gifted, talented, successful.

These so-called communicators genuinely believe they are getting away with it. Bearing witness to a competitor one day almost contorting himself to find ways to drop names of prominent clients, confident that his skills of salesmanship are serving him brilliantly, we watch as the prospective client does as we do.

He raises an eyebrow, as if to suggest, "And you think I am *fooled?*"

It does not work.

However you do it, when you flash your writer's underwear, you're naked. You have exposed yourself. You've communicated only that you are eager to impress and not adept at hiding it.

Don't try to show off; since we were kids, we've been able to detect that a mile away.

Don't talk to, talk with: Communicate.

The Brand Called You

One of the mantras of the decade has involved branding individuals the way you brand a can of soda pop.

It's not hard to immediately recognize a slight flaw in this thinking. A can of Pepsi-Cola contains four major ingredients. A human being contains, for starters, forty-six chromosomes and so much nuance that while all cans of Pepsi-Cola are the same, not even the fingerprints of any two people in the world are identical.

We experience cars and cans of cola differently from how we experience people. That dictates that the principles of marketing people are very different.

In plotting the Brand Called You, too many people believe they can weave a tale. They believe in magic, or that brands are produced through cleverness and deception. Perhaps they think of examples like Volkswagen, and decide that clever advertising made the aptly nicknamed Volkswagen Bug adorable and desirable, and take that as evidence of marketing's ability to deceive. Perhaps they are among many people who think that cars are just cars, and that any mystique surrounding one must have been artificially created.

So we either rebel at the idea of branding, or we embrace it as a useful tool of deception.

Great brands, however, are authentic. They have endured because people have learned they are credible and have come to trust those brands to be what they say they are; great brands have integrity. What they say is *integrated*—integrated and integrity are related expressions—with what they do.

No one responds to our efforts to be other than who we are. They respond to the good but bad, excellent but flawed person across the table from them.

A Brand Called You suggests that you can spin yourself, not unlike the tale of Rumpelstiltskin turning straw into gold. Myth and folklore are filled with failed examples of this attempt, of which none may be more memorable than *The Wizard of Oz*.

The Wizard had fame and power; he could inspire dread in lions, scarecrows, and the entire land of Oz. His attempt at creating the Wizard brand succeeded for some time, until someone—

and it wasn't hard to figure—reacted to him as the young boy did to the Emperor with No Clothes.

Build an authentic brand; there is no other kind.

Inspirations for Your Brand

Consider two of the world's great brands: Nike and Harley-Davidson.

Faced with the challenge of the long-established but arguably long-in-the-tooth German company Adidas, Phil Knight—a true American original—assembled a similarly minded group of West Coast rebels. Together they created a company like no other before or since.

From its beginnings, Nike reveled in its strangeness and proclaimed it publicly. (A memorable early ad showed several sloppily clad employees sprawled across the seats in an airport, while another depicted a fellow who appeared to be a refugee from Ken Kesey's Merry Pranksters, above the headline, "Our first employee is still with us. We think.")

Nike stayed true to its rebel beginnings. It ran commercials featuring Charles Barkley insisting he was not, and would not be, a role model—a bold suggestion. They ran ads of the young Tiger Woods announcing he was ready for the world. But as a black golfer, he asked us back, "Are you ready for me?"

Harley never pretended to be something other than a Hog, a motorcycle you could barely budge if you turned one over. Harley never celebrated its endorsement by the Hells Angels, but never shied from that connection, either.

When the Japanese invaded America with lighter bikes that flew down highways and flew out of dealerships, Harley stayed true to Harley. It remained authentic, cherishing its past. And as its brand inspired devotion, it reminded all of us of just how intense brand devotion can be—if you are authentic.

In a memorable full-color, two-page-spread advertisement, Harley showcased a familiar icon. It was a close-up photo of a thick, tanned male biceps emblazoned with a multicolored tattoo: the

Harley logo. Below the photo the copywriter Ron Sackett had crafted this memorable line:

"When was the last time you felt this passionately about *anything*?"

Like shoes and motorcycles, like us; we establish our brands in the world. We succeed only by being true to ourselves.

People have developed nearly faultless detectors for the fake and the contrived. You can fool some of them some of the time.

But eventually, they figure it—and you—out.

A life in marketing confirms the wisdom of to thine own self be true. Ultimately, it will feel more comfortable for you; you don't have to think about how you want to be seen. Being authentic works better for you, too: you earn trust and comfort, the keys to enduring relationships.

You have a brand. Make sure yours is honest.

Apple's Wisdom:
Look for Metaphors

In a complex world, describing what you do or
sell has become more complicated, too. Ask
someone to explain a defined benefits plan and its
benefits, for example. Before your eyes, the listener's eyes glaze over with puzzlement.

Want to make yourself more appealing?

Imitate Apple.

Apple once offered several products that were
useful, even powerful, in business settings. But the
company encountered two obstacles.

First, people considered Apple computers to be
"home computers"—more like toys than serious
business tools, more for amateurs than serious
professionals. No matter how much function,
power, and memory Apple added to their computers, they could not answer, "What difference
can an Apple computer make for my business?"

Business users felt content with their IBMs and
IBM clones.

What difference *could* Apple make?

Apple found its answer in a perfect metaphor.

It was "Desktop Publishing."

Prospects got it. Moreover, prospects believed that no other company offered this capability, because none mentioned it. Because prospects closely associated Apple with words and graphics, as opposed to numbers and spreadsheets, Apple also sounded like the ideal tool for Desktop Publishing, even if its competitors could assemble "Desktop Publishing Solutions."

And note quickly here a subtle but important point: Apple's omission of the word "solutions." By the late 1980s, "solutions" had become the most familiar buzz word in American business. Within months it seemed that every company— including those offering spray painters and garden hose accessories—now offered this New Thing called "solutions."

The problem with "solutions"—easily overlooked—is that the term implies complexity. It's plural, for one thing. "There is no one answer," the term tells us, "there are many." The prospects know they must consider a variety of products and services to see which combination might work best.

"Solutions" promised complexity, when what people crave is simplicity.

Apple didn't offer many things: it offered a simple, wonderful metaphor: Desktop Publishing.

(Note the effect: Desktop Publishing implies a single, simple "solution." "Solutions" suggests many.)

What metaphor will make your message more vivid?

Inspirations for Metaphors

A successful human resources consultant refers to himself as "an HR internist." He assesses a company's human resources, immediately identifies any illnesses, and prescribes proven cures.

NameLab quickly and cleverly suggests that the firm take a scientific approach, and perhaps a more proven approach, to developing company names.

Geoffrey Moore chose *Crossing the Chasm* as his vivid metaphor for his book describing the challenge of going from selling complex products to techies, for whom nothing is too complex, to selling them to people like us, who abhor complexity and still use only 10 percent of the functions of our DVD players.

(Geoffrey himself once suggested that a vivid metaphor can be worth 40,000 pages of analysis. *Chasm*'s sales seems to confirm his point.)

Consider the best-selling books of a year ago: *The Tipping Point. Blink. The World Is Flat.* Compare the power of those metaphors to the non-metaphorical titles that convey the same thing: *Points of Accelerated Market Adoption. Immediate Judgments. A Truly Global World.*

The metaphorical titles themselves suggest that even though their material is identical, the books are different.

Among other promises your metaphor can make, it promises that your communications will be clearer, more vivid, and more engaging—a worthwhile promise to a prospect all by itself, in this age of confusion.

For inspiration, look all around you.

Don't Make Me Laugh

Your friend tells you an unfunny joke. You laugh anyway.

That's natural. You are being kind.

But when you send someone a clever self-promotion, encouraged by the handful of people who smiled when you proposed it, something different happens.

You send out a package to a prospect. You enclose a plastic bee inside, for example, and attach to it the note, "Heard the buzz?"

You call a recipient. "Did you get my little package?" She answers yes, and adds, "It was cute." Adding that comment to your friend's apparent reassurances that your bee is a good idea, you decide that it must be. Psychologists have named your error. It's called a false consensus effect: the habit of assuming others agree with us when they do not.

You keep trying the gimmick.

But your basic message is, "Try me, I'm clever." Many people will feel uncomfortable with your implication: that they lack sophistication, are easily fooled, and may even be frivolous.

A gimmick also makes it appear that you have nothing important to say, so you are relying on bad puns, word play, and tricks instead.

If you worry, "Is my idea professional?," it probably isn't.

Touting Your Credentials

You worked hard for your achievements.

You have reason to be proud, and to assume others will value them, too.

They will—but far less than you suspect.

Again, consider the research that studied the effect of experts' credentials on jurors. Do people place more faith in the expert with the more impressive credentials—the "better" school, higher degree, longer list of articles in respected publications?

They don't. They place faith in the person who communicates most clearly.

Why stress something that matters relatively little?

Perhaps worse, you may sound immodest. Touting sounds like tooting one's horn, which tends to repel people.

More important, consider the phrase "What have you done for me lately?" Your credentials come from your past, and in other's minds may reveal little about your ability to answer their needs.

Be careful in complimenting yourself.

Don't Pitch;
Weave

Think of an eighteen-month-old child, and listen carefully.

Our language reflects who we are and how we

think. It clearly reveals how others respond to what you say—and how best to say it.

Listen to children of eighteen months. They use only a few words, and their words reveal what they love. With some exceptions, for example, young boys quickly learn the names of more than a dozen vehicles. Before he can say "flower," he is apt to know truck, bus, cab, bicycle, car, van, tractor, and a dozen other things on wheels.

Wherever you go and whatever the child's gender, one word pops from children's mouths at a startlingly early age.

It's "story."

You can be startled to hear "story" at first, because it's not easy for a child to articulate. At the time a child first uses the word, the only other two-syllable words they usually have learned are the two obvious choices: Mommy and Daddy.

Mommy, Daddy, then story. (Ask South Americans if their children show this preference, too, and they will nod: "*Mamá*, *papá*, and *cuento*.")

Why so early? Because stories are how we come to understand our world at every age. Our lives are stories. The evening news, television shows, movies, and plays: all are stories. The music we love tells its story through lyrics, or evokes them with its words.

Stories give us context, and context helps everyone at every age understand.

Stories wield special power because they can be translated quickly into something visual. When we hear a story, we see it, too, and the visual image becomes something that sticks in our memories long after the words have fled.

We say that when we understand something, we "see" it; stories create in our mind's eye pictures that we see.

This prompts the question:

Why, when people sell, do they list their achievements rather than tell their stories?

Why do so many firms spend so much time saying how good they are, and so little time telling their stories?

A financial advisor lists for a prospect his firm's array of services: insurance, estate planning, variable annuities, defined benefit plans, mutual funds, stocks, and bonds. There is this service and that, and such a record of growth and achievement.

At the end of all of this, what is the prospect thinking?

"What's a variable annuity?"

She thinks, "I don't know what all of those things are. I am confused, frightened, and overwhelmed." She does know that she has three kids approaching college age, x dollars in savings, y dollars in a mortgage, and a current income of z. So her question for you is simple:

How can you help me?

Have you done that already, for someone like me?

Tell me your story.

Tell stories.

What's "A Good Story"?

Think of Bambi, Holly Golightly, or Holden Caulfield.

For that matter, even think of Cartman in *South Park*, Snoopy in *Peanuts*, or Spider-Man in all his incarnations.

All good stories have a hero, and two other key elements you should incorporate in yours:

1. A serious challenge.
2. The hero dealing with the challenge and learning something as a result.

It's easy to see why most company's stories fail. Try this story from a typical brochure:

"In 1955, we began business as Acme Tool & Die. Today, we are a thriving company with offices in thirteen countries and over $1.5 billion in annual revenues. We are ISO-9000 certified, and regularly mentioned among the 'Best Companies to Work For' in the world."

It's an impressive story, in one sense. There's only one problem:

It is not a good story.

It has the wrong hero.

If you want your prospect to identify with your story, you must do what great storytellers do: make that person identify with your hero.

Your prospect is not going to identify with you, your company, or its products for a simple reason. You are not, and never can be, their hero.

Instead, they are their heroes. People identify with themselves; they want solutions to their problems. They are not interested in helping you reach $1.6 billion in annual revenues or opening an office in Shanghai.

They are interested in making their own lives, somehow, better.

The ideal story talks about a client, not about the company. It puts the listener in that hero's shoes, and creates tension around some challenge that faced the hero: a health problem, financial issues, some great but unfulfilled desire. The good story shows how the person overcame those challenges; it has a happy ending.

Your best stories are not about you; they are about *them*. Tell stories that make your clients the heroes, and make your prospects identify with them.

Then they will see how you can help them.

Put the audience, not you, in the hero's shoes.

The First Trick in Storytelling

"I've often wondered what goes into a hot dog. Now I know and I wish I didn't."

"It was the best of times, it was the worst of times . . ."

"Happy families are all alike; every unhappy family is unhappy in its own way."

These are the vital words in three different but wonderfully told stories: "Block That Chicken-furter," a column in *Life* magazine by the wonderful writer and writing teacher William Zinsser; *A Tale of Two Cities*, by Charles Dickens; and *Anna Karenina*, by Leo Tolstoy.

They are the leads.

Each lead pulls us immediately into each story. Each provokes us with a question. And each assures us we are in good hands: the hands of someone who will engage us for the rest of his story.

Your key sentence in every presentation is your first. Your first sentence must make your listeners eager to hear your second; your second must make them as eager to hear your third.

Expressed another way, the first fifteen words are as important as the next fifteen hundred.

How do you write this most important sentence? *Carefully.* Give listeners a compelling reason to listen, but without giving away your ending. Too often a presenter reveals her ending. Like audiences for movies, listeners to presentations lose interest in a story when they know its ending.

As models, consider two strong leads from two recent presentations.

"Anyone who questions the power of a brand,"

the presenter begins, "surely has not considered the comical story of Rogaine."

"The copy needed some spice, I realized," the presenter begins, "so I did the obvious: I threw in a pterodactyl."

If you spend three hours writing your presentations, spend thirty minutes writing your leads.

Grab them immediately; craft your leads.

The Second Trick in Storytelling

"Let me tell you a good story about certificates of deposit."

No, don't.

Our stories in business, no matter how artfully we tell them, invariably lack the elements of the great stories that captivate readers: villains, treachery and violence, sex and romance. All spun with vivid imaginations, stories with these elements naturally engage listeners more than stories about variable annuities, angioplasty catheters, and IT consulting.

Keeping your listeners' interest takes even more effort, because your listeners know they are being sold rather than entertained. They know your ending in one sense:

You want to sell them something.

This doesn't mean, however, that you abandon the devices of good storytelling. To the contrary: *It means you must make even better use of them.*

That leads to the second trick in storytelling: the Next Lead.

You open with a strong lead. Then you provide some detail that keeps the listener interested. You provide more detail. Now, like a piece of music, your story is ebbing downward and your audience is ebbing with it. You need a jump-start.

You need the Next Lead.

Just as your lead grabs your audience and "leads" them into your story, you periodically need to reclaim their attention.

The Next Lead resembles the first. You might think of it as the classic infomercial gambit that works so well, so much so that people spoof it: "But Wait, There's More!!"

Some examples:

"They hoped to hit $5 million in their fifth year. They hit $7 million. The story of how they did that, you will see, is even more intriguing . . ."

"But the best part of the story is what happened next . . ."

"As if the flood wasn't bad enough, lightning struck them again a week later in more violent form: a visit from the IRS . . ." (We said business stories lack sex and violence, but you find plenty of use for horror.)

The Next Lead prompts your audience to rise up again and ask, "Now what?"

When you rehearse presentations in front of others, ask them, "Where could this use a lift?" Insert a Next Lead there.

Craft one Next Lead—then at least one more.

Work the Message

You know the problem. You read it every day.

You receive a communication promoting something: a cell phone service, a new restaurant, a wonder vitamin.

You quickly toss it aside.

But perhaps one day, you enter the office of a consultant. The packaging for his message is modest, but its message is compelling.

"Each of our consultants left one of our industry's four largest firms to join us, and none have left us. And in that period, every client has stayed."

Find your message, keep it simple, and repeat it often.

The Talent of the Clarifiers

Great communicators are skilled editors. Like author Elmore Leonard, they know to slash the parts that readers skip anyway.

Editors take the time to edit, and by taking the time, communicate to their reader, "You are important to me."

Mark Twain expressed the vital role of editing when he wrote a letter to a friend. Nearing the end, Twain realized the number of words in the letter far exceeded the number of ideas, and that he had presented his reader with a bit of a task. So Twain expressed both his apologies and his understanding of the burdens of editing with a final note:

"I'd have written a shorter letter but I didn't have enough time."

Revise every memo. Then revise it again. Read it aloud and ask, "How can this be said more succinctly?" Brevity is power.

Read it aloud; revise it again.

Making Yourself Clear

At least half of every document is clear.

The problem? The other half.

The even slightly fuzzy parts make your reader second-guess the clear parts. Your reader thought she understood, but your other verbiage now makes it unclear. The fuzzy part seems to contradict the clear part—or does it?

Suddenly, she isn't sure there *is* a clear part.

A simple technique will help you write with greater clarity, which in turn, makes your readers more confident and more apt to consider you an expert.

Cut every document in half.

Your Last Step

Read everything you write aloud.

Your ear will pick up the mistakes that your eyes missed. Your ear will read the document the way your recipient hears it, too. If you proofread only with your eyes, your eyes will deceive you because they know what you said. They will tend to see what you think you wrote, rather than the actual words on the paper.

When you read aloud, you hear the mistakes.

Your ears, being musical, also will hear awkward rhythms. Smooth those out and your copy will flow for the reader. The reader will read more easily, enjoy the ride, and appreciate the person who provided it.

After you write something, be sure to hear it.

TWO KEY SKILLS: LISTENING AND SPEAKING

How to Be
Fascinating

We recently spoke to a colleague who had attended a party a week earlier. The day after the party, a woman to whom he had spoken sent him an e-mail of thanks. "I thoroughly enjoyed our conversation," she wrote.

The next day the fellow learned that the woman had spoken to a mutual friend, and told her our colleague was "a wonderful conversationalist. *So* interesting!"

Interesting, indeed.

The fellow said he spoke for not more than one minute. She had spoken the other fifty.

Listening makes you captivating.

The Ears Have It

Our vocabulary constantly reveals how we think.

Consider what we say about talk.

"Talk is cheap." "That's mere rhetoric." "That's just a lot of verbiage."

Now listen to what else we say.

"Silence is golden."

These expressions reveal our beliefs: we think people speak too much and listen too little. We mistrust words, but we trust—and we praise—listeners.

"She's a great listener." "He really listened to me."

Businesses often run ads that feature the claim "We listen." They assume we value their listening because it means that the company will hear what the client needs and will provide an excellent solution. Hence,

"Better solutions through better listening."

These businesses and their ads miss most of the point. You can listen to clients and still be unclear what they want, not least of all because truly smart listening requires truly smart questioning. Not easy.

We don't value people who listen because they will respond with answers. When a friend listens to our issues, for example, we do not value that she responded with a suggestion.

We value that she cared enough to listen.

Just hearing ourselves articulate our problems gives us clarity—as modern psychology obviously realizes, from its emphasis on revelation-based therapy. As in that therapy, the speaker values not just the listener's answer, but the listener's attention. It is satisfying just to be heard.

Struck by the rapid rise of Ben Taylor, who came to America from Africa and soon was running a major ExecuTrain franchise, an advice seeker asked him his key to success. Without a split-second pause, Taylor answered:

"I listen."

Some simple advice helped propel Ruth Ann Marshall to the top of her profession, the presidency of MasterCard International. When asked to reflect on her life's great lessons, Ruth recalled her mother's advice:

"You have two ears and one mouth, Ruth Ann. That means you should listen twice as much as you speak."

Listen. Actively and often; always.

The Easiest Way to Lose Someone

Years ago, an accomplished surgeon was asked what was missing in his life.

Like so many profound statements, the importance of his answer didn't make sense until years later. "I'd like to take a safari to Africa," he said. "But there's no other one thing I need or want, and I have all the money I will ever spend.

"The thing I covet most, and miss most, is time."

We measure friends in just this way. We measure our importance to them in time. Acquaintances give us moments; friends give us hours; good friends give us days.

Others will regard you in direct proportion to how you appear to regard them. The critical word here is "appear," and another story illustrates this, and the value of time.

She should have been a star. Every early indication was that she would be. By thirty-three she was named her company's regional director of sales. Forty-five people reported to her. Her energy, charm, attention to detail, and ability to sell made her rapid ascent seem inevitable.

Ten years later, she was looking for work. Two years after that she was looking again, dealt another blow by her fatal yet fixable flaw.

You could see it early. The source of the flaw was innocent: she was anxious.

But it was not her anxiety that doomed her. It was its by-product. Wherever she was, she was in a hurry. She not only struggled to sit still, but struggled to focus on people with whom she was speaking. A distraction entered—a person entered the room, an idea entered her head. She attended to the distraction and disconnected from the person.

She was unaware of what she projected. No one ever pointed it out.

Instead, people simply came to feel unimportant to her. Clients who had signed on, signed off. Colleagues who had been impressed by her energy were hurt by how little she seemed to reserve for them.

People did matter to her. She knew that; close friends knew that, too. But the first rule of sales and marketing is not "You are who you are." It is "You are who you appear to be."

Early in her career, and early in a meeting with her, people she encountered wrote off her lack of attention to them as energy and drive, and tolerated it. But as time passed, they lost their patience, and she lost ground.

You are who you appear to be. And she appeared, too often, to be someone interested in anything other than everyone else.

She should have learned a rule: the Rule of the Second.

When you listen to someone, pause a full second before replying. It signals that you have listened. If you start speaking immediately, you create a perception that you have been waiting for the person to stop so you could get to the important part: your words, your thoughts.

Before you speak, take one second.

Our Misunderstanding About Listening

"I'm not doing much right now, just listening to something."

That statement illuminates our problem. We view talking and listening differently. We view speaking as an *activity;* we are *active* in doing it, even animated. Some successful speakers even appear hyperactive.

But what is listening?

We think listening is passive. All we need to do is just sit and listen. We assume that works.

It does not, as college classes reveal.

A college student certainly can attend classes, merely listen, and try to rely on memory later when the exam is given. Most students know better, however. They take notes. Far from being passive, they are more active than the speaker, who is single-tasking: speaking. The students are both listening and writing, and in some cases, reading what they have just written.

Their experience reminds us that successful listening is active. You must engage yourself.

But you cannot take notes. So what do you do?

The closest best thing: form visual images of what the speaker is saying. If she's describing crewing a boat on the Cape, picture her on a wind-buffeted sailboat skipping along the whitecaps. If she describes friends from Florida, picture palm trees to help you absorb and recall that detail.

We do not remember words well. We remember images.

Listen in images and you will listen far better, and your obvious attention will compliment the speaker.

Listen actively, in pictures.

One More Step

Psychologists know that our bodies reflect our thoughts. If we feel sad, for example, we tend to slump our shoulders and bow our heads.

The reverse turns out to be true, too. Our minds follow our bodies. Voluntarily slump your shoulders and bow your head, and your thoughts will turn toward sadness.

Listening works this way, too. An effective device for listening better is literally this: *Put your entire body into it.* Feel your entire body, from head to hands to feet, engaging the speaker. When you engage your body in engaging the speaker, your mind engages more, too.

And again, the speaker will notice, and appreciate the regard that you are showing.

Put your entire body into it.

Listen to What Isn't Said

Most of what people think is unknown to them. It is subconscious. They do not articulate it and often cannot.

This has one enormous implication that partly contradicts advice you will hear throughout your life: listen. The problem with this advice is that when you listen, all you hear is what people know and are willing to say.

At best, this is only 10 percent of the story.

If all you did is listen, all you will know is what they said.

You cannot merely listen. *You must observe.* Life is not words; it is actions. How do they act?

What does she do? Where does she spend her time and money? What does her posture tell you? What does her bookshelf say?

Listen to words, but then use your eyes: See what they're saying, too.

Proof That Listening Works

Survivor.

Our friend and future best-selling author Jacob Greene recently reminded us of its importance.

If you can endure the commercials and the high camp, the program reveals plenty about the art of winning friends and influencing people.

By the end of each series, when only two or three people remain, guess who is one of them?

The Listener. The one who stays up late listening to the guy who misses his kids back home or the woman who can't stand Monica's whining.

Everyone else gets thrown off the island, but the Listener sticks.

Listeners win.

The Heart of Every Presentation

His Stanford students still remember Ron Rebholz.

At first, few were excited to hear from Ron. He was going to talk for three months about Shakespeare. What little Shakespeare the college students already had read in high school seemed written in another tongue.

They could roughly decipher the lines in *Romeo and Juliet*, "Sin from my lips? Oh trespass, sweetly urged! Give me my sin again!" for example. It had to do with kissing, and possibly more. Otherwise, the Bard's words baffled them.

So few were excited on that sunny fall day

many years ago when Mr. Rebholz took the stage, and they prepared to satisfy the school's requirement that they take a literature class.

Within minutes, all that changed. They were excited—no, enthralled—because Rebholz was. At the very least, each of them could tell—because this man obviously felt it deeply—that Shakespeare really mattered. The students sensed that if they could hold out, read carefully, and look past the quaintness of Shakespeare's language to the enduring truths they conveyed, their lives might be changed.

Where would they feel that change? Where it matters most: in their spirits.

No presentation that you give—whether it's about Hamlet or the need for better traffic signals at the corner of First and Main—will succeed solely on its merits. You often think you have made your material interesting and spoken well. But only when you feel, and feel the difference that acting on our words will make, do others respond.

Their heads go nowhere until their hearts lead them there.

You learn this if you speak often. In your first presentations, you make sure every argument is airtight, every fact well presented, all your logic irrefutable. Then you close, walk from the podium—and realize nothing has changed.

Another phenomenon illustrates this point. It's the experience of many people who speak often over many years. Eventually, someone approaches them after a speech and, in the course of conversation, says, "You are an excellent motivational speaker."

Many speakers feel wounded when they hear that. All that work and study, they decide, and I'm just one of those hand-wavers you see on television, bouncing across a stage like a high school cheerleader? Not long after that, however, they realize what an effective presentation actually communicates.

They realize a great presentation *must* be motivational.

A wonderful observation about teaching captures this idea: "A poor teacher describes; a good teacher explains; an excellent teacher demonstrates; a great teacher *inspires*."

Regardless of what any effective presentation says, what it conveys is that its subject *matters*; it matters to you to retain my services, read this article I read, consider voting for my candidate. And where does it matter?

In the heart and soul. Great presentations are not intellectual; they are spiritual. You must reach the heart and soul.

Effective financial planners do not sell you on

quadrupling your money in twenty-five years; they sell you the *feeling* you will experience when you do.

College football recruiters do not sell young men nine wins, two losses, and the chance to play in televised bowl games. They sell the *feeling* of being among people you like, of hearing the echoes in your helmet from the cheers of 80,000 fans, and all the other sensations summarized in a feeling every football player knows: the sensation that one observer called "the thrill of the grass."

(Please know: No one can adequately explain this feeling, but few feelings equal it.)

Every great presentation motivates.

The Role of Eloquence

You know this; you've heard it.

A speaker rises, speaks eloquently, conveys intelligence and understanding, and sits. You are impressed but unmoved. Weeks later, another speaker rises.

It has always been this way. Centuries ago it was perfectly illustrated by two Greek generals, Aeschines and Demosthenes. As David Ogilvy later observed in his classic *Confessions of an Advertising Man*, Aeschines spoke brilliantly—to his detriment. Listeners raved at his eloquence.

Demosthenes, by contrast, stumbled over many words, even rambled at times. No one marveled at his skill. But everyone was moved by his passion. So the listeners admired and applauded Aeschines.

But when Demosthenes spoke, they turned to each other and shouted, "We Must March Against Phillip!"

The eloquent speaker impresses us, but does not move us to act. We are not moved because the speaker appears not to be. If this does not truly matter to the speaker, we decide, why should it matter to me?

Don't impress them; move them.

How to Keep Advancing

Bob Boylan once wrote a chapter for a book on leadership entitled "The Leading Role Is Always a Speaking Part."

He was right. The leaders of everything, and in everything, speak. Speaking is considered both a sign and an obligation of leadership. True leaders acquire knowledge and share it.

Eventually, then, your career path arrives at a critical point: the intersection of "Speak" and "Don't Speak."

Speak heads due north. It's upward.

Don't Speak takes a sharp right turn and heads laterally.

You certainly can choose the easier path. Like all paths of less resistance, however, it does not go far. And walking along it brings few rewards.

Start preparing today for your arrival at this intersection.

Head north, starting now.

Reaching an Audience

You don't reach your audience.

You reach the people, one at a time.

If an audience responds to you, it's because almost every person in the audience does individually. Each responds because you reached each one directly, and specifically.

You reach each member the way you reach any person: you look that person in the eyes. Your eyes, as they say, are the windows to your soul.

Your eyes tell them who you are, and you are what you are selling.

Talk to one, not many, from your eyes to theirs.

In Your Eyes

At every moment in a business relationship, you are doing just what that term suggests: relating.

You are not relating to a person if you are focused on a page, reading from a presentation.

Nor are you relating if you are focused on a screen, reading from PowerPoint.

Or looking at one side of the room, but rarely the other.

Or looking at a few people, but not at everyone.

Each time you look away, you invite the listeners to look away, too. Each time you look away, you invite the instinctive response, "What is this person hiding?"

"Why is she afraid to look at me?"

Students of body language learn that only pathological liars can look a person in the eyes when they lie. We all know this instinctively; that's why we use a common phrase when we fear someone isn't telling us the truth:

"Look me in the eyes and say that." To inspire trust, you must look people in the eyes.

Look them in the eyes. Constantly.

How to Give an Excellent Ten-Minute Speech

Write a twenty-minute speech.

Cut out the weakest half: the weakest stories, the unnecessary words—your least favorite half.

Then cut out a minute, and give a nine-minute speech.

You will deliver with more intensity and energy, because you have less time. That will make you more inspiring.

Your material will sound more interesting and compelling.

Best of all, your audience will be thrilled you finished a bit early. They will decide that you are organized, succinct, confident, and respectful of their time. You will keep their meeting on time, or help them make up time they have lost, which meetings always need.

They will feel you came to respect their needs rather than satisfy your ego.

You will, in short, make several good impressions.

In speaking, as in so many things in life, less is more.

How to Give an Excellent Thirty-Minute Speech

Speak for twenty-two minutes.

Why Speeches Must Be Short

Because people have less time, and have learned they can get valuable information in minutes.

They also have been conditioned by television. Every twelve minutes a commercial allows them to take a break. This has conditioned them to twelve-minute bites.

You hear a hint of people's value of brevity in another familiar phrase: "short and sweet.

To audiences, short *is* sweet.

Keep it short.

Bringing in the
Back of the Room

Sometimes, you need to look all the way to the trees. With a little practice, you can.

Great performers have this gift, which was vividly demonstrated at the Greek Theatre in Los Angeles in the summer of 1968.

The great performer was the singer Harry Belafonte. Even the oh-so-hip, too-cool-for-calypso, *Sgt. Pepper*–era college students in the audience felt Belafonte's magic.

To appreciate his gift, picture an outdoor amphitheater with rows reaching back almost as far as you could see. Look up, and you see above and behind the amphitheater another row: the thick oak trees that line the back of the theater.

Look a little closer, and you realize the trees are not alone.

They are occupied. At least fifty people are sitting in them to watch Belafonte perform.

You might never have noticed the tree dwellers if Mr. Belafonte had not called out to them several times. With his unique affection and charm, Mr.

Belafonte would banter with this group, for whom he had coined a special name: the Scholies.

They were the college students on scholarships who could not afford even back row seats. But they climbed the trees with glee so they could witness this rare performer. He was touched, and touched them back.

In speaking, you might hear this referred to as "bringing in the back of the room." Wherever you go, whether to a large party or a large presentation, bring in the entire room—beginning at the back.

This is not "working a room," or making yourself its center—even when, as in a presentation, you literally are standing center stage. The best performers and most effective people bring others to the center stage, even while they are standing on it.

To witness this firsthand, find a television listing and learn the next time that the comedienne Paula Poundstone is featured (typically on Comedy Central, of course). Paula possesses the gift of being able to extemporize, hilariously, in a literal split second. But you will notice, too, how she brings others to the front.

By reaching out to make the crowd part of her presentation, she creates a special experience.

You can and should do this, too.

Even when you have the stage—indeed, especially then—share it.

The generosity, warmth, and the sense of human connection makes a good moment better, and makes you dramatically more effective.

Look to the trees.

Jokes

After attending a few speeches you may come away thinking there is a cardinal rule:

Start with a joke. Apparently, it warms up your audience.

Armed with this insight, you search for some jokes. When called upon to speak, you trot out a couple of these gems. Your audience laughs, confirming that this technique works.

It rarely does.

The audience laughs. They laugh not because they want to, but because you want them to. They also laugh because they admire your willingness to take the podium at all; fear of speaking ranks as the world's number one phobia, ahead of dying and snakes. Your audience members don't want you to feel paralyzed from the beginning, as they would.

So they chuckle to give you strength.

They laugh, too, because our culture has conditioned them to. From childhood they've heard laugh tracks on every situation comedy and learned, "Joke, then laugh."

When you try to tell jokes, however, you cross a field of land mines. When you attempt a joke, you are competing in your audience's minds with Chris Rock, Larry the Cable Guy, and Ellen DeGeneres, who appear on television every day and night. These professionals have practiced for thousands of hours.

They have perfected running; you have just taken up crawling.

More important, when people hear these comedians, they never suspect the comedian is telling someone else's joke. The comedians are telling their stories. They are relating their own experiences and point of view. They are telling you who they are, what they think, how they believe.

That engages you; you are interested in others, partly because they teach you about yourself.

When you tell a joke you have found, you are not revealing yourself. You merely are repeating someone else's joke. To make it worse, most speakers pretend their jokes actually do involve them. "My wife yesterday says to me, Frank . . ." The listeners follow the story to the end, then realize it was too funny to have really happened to that amateur; no one's spouse is *that* funny.

These listeners decide, at least subconsciously, that the speaker has opened with a trick. They feel deceived.

You can't compete with professionals, and you can't afford to appear deceptive.

Beware of jokes.

The One Joke That Works

Blonde jokes, Polish jokes, Aggie jokes—an endless list; too many jokes come at others' expense.

In fact, it's been said that for every ten jokes, a person makes a hundred enemies.

Audiences do, however, love one particular joke at the expense of someone:

They love when you poke fun at yourself.

When you bring yourself down, you bring yourself from behind the podium and onto the floor. You announce, "I am up here, but I really am with you."

In searching for humor, look at your life. Most of the great modern comics are *observational;* they merely look around and see how profoundly silly, absurd, funny, or merely human we—and they—can be.

People love the humor of everyday life, because it is theirs, too. They deeply appreciate those who can find it. Your wit provides them a clue to your warmth and lets them peek inside you. Jokes, by contrast, merely tell them that you found a joke book and memorized one or two.

Let your jokes be on you.

The Perils of PowerPoint

Armed with the information—provided by manufacturers—that human beings remember what they see far better than what they hear, American businesspeople have transformed the country.

We now live in PowerPoint Nation.

And we've created a problem, as the following stories illustrate.

Beware of slides.

Aids to Understanding?

A multinational, Colorado-based company changed its name in 2002. After three years of solid growth, they decided to find out how they were really doing.

They particularly wanted to know, "Are we better known, and if so, for what?"

Both answers disappointed them.

When researchers asked potential prospects, "What companies are you aware of in this industry?" surprisingly few named the Coloradans. When researchers prompted the survey subjects with the company's name, a three-letter acronym, the response still was disappointing. Too few prospects recognized the name.

What did these potential prospects recognize? With a frequency as surprising as their silence about the name, they answered:

"The Globe."

The company used a blue globe as its symbol. The globe, smaller than the name, was rendered in blue. The company name was rendered in a more conspicuous bold black. Surely the name was more memorable than a symbol as common as a globe!

But it was not.

Why did prospects remember the globe but not the name? After all, they read and heard the name more often than saw the globe, and the name appeared larger and more conspicuous. And the name was "visual." Prospects saw the name depicted, or so you would argue, "visually."

They could not remember the name because words are *not* visuals; words are words. Studies show that we remember words best by translating them into visuals. When we hear "donkey," for example, we do not see the letters d,o,n,k,e,y.

We see the animal instead.

For the same reason, we struggle to remember collections of letters, because we cannot visualize them. We remember "penguin," for example, because we can picture one. But we cannot remember PNG or the phrase "regulatory environment handicapping efforts."

This brings us to the fallacy of the PowerPoint presentation. We assume that if a presenter reinforces a message with a slide with key words, we remember the message better. We don't, because words aren't visual.

Flash a globe and people remember it. Flash a set of words and they forget.

Beware of visual aids.

Visual Aids, Yes. Memory Aids, No

It happened at a national sales meeting in Atlanta, but it undoubtedly occurred that day in Houston, Detroit, and even Dubrovnik.

A national sales director for a Fortune 200 company was reviewing a great year and previewing the next one. He was amply armed with slides that faded and dissolved, spiraled and cut-and-pasted, and displayed striking bar graphs and pie charts in a dozen bright colors.

At the end of his presentation, two researchers stopped four attendees to test their thesis. Having seen the slides in advance, the pair decided to test how well the slides had communicated.

They asked the attendees, "What were the key obstacles in South America? What were the top- and bottom-selling products? What was the projected revenue increase for the next year?"

The attendees correctly answered 30 percent of the questions—but then, they knew several of those answers before the presentation. None of the four people could name more than one obstacle; the presenter had mentioned five.

Yet the sales director had presented the information "visually"; he had used *visual* aids. The prospects should have retained 70 percent of the information, if studies on visually aided memory are true. Those studies may be reliable, but they apply to "visual information": to images, rather than collections of letters, words, and numbers on a screen.

But there's more. The researchers went one step further. They asked the presenter the same questions.

He knew many of the answers, as he should have. But remarkably, he could name the best- and worst-selling products (human beings tend to remember the extreme but not the more ordinary), but gave the wrong order for the remaining five products. His explanation was simple, but revealing.

"I've got all that information in my slides."

Think of what he said. He said he did not need to know the information because he already had it. But he hadn't stored it in his mind, where it might influence and inform his decisions. He had it in slides, packed away behind his file cabinet.

Not only do we mistakenly rely on slides to help us deliver our messages, but we believe that creating our slides leaves us with the necessary knowledge. "I know and understand this material," we assume, "because I put it all in slides."

Slides, it appears, do not just fail the listeners. They fail the speakers, too.

Visual aids regularly diminish everyone's understanding of the material.

Where Slides Fail Most Vividly

We have saved the strongest for last.

Slides do not fail us only because they tend to produce presentations that fail to engage the listeners with the material and with the presenter, both of which are critical to a presentation's effectiveness.

Slides cheat us because they deprive presentations of what makes a presentation most effective: a heart.

A vivid illustration of this comes from New Orleans, in the wake of its disaster in 2005. In Katrina's aftermath, everyone looked back and said that everyone knew what was coming.

Yet they didn't.

To understand how this could occur, imagine listening to a presentation on New Orleans's emergency preparedness, six months before Hurricane Katrina.

Imagine seeing this slide:

Issues of Concern:

- 1. Adequacy of Levees
- 2. Backflow into Pontchartrain
- 3. Other Infrastructure Issues

You immediately feel the problem. The city's survival, as we later learned to our horror, represented a matter of life and death. But is that danger, that emotion, or that risk conveyed in this slide?

To the contrary, *it is obliterated by it.*

Ask meeting hosts what they want from a presentation. They want emotional resonance. They want people to be inspired, motivated, entertained; they want the words to pass through the ears of the attendees and alight in their souls.

Far from encouraging this, a slide presentation compels the creator to fashion data points bereft of any emotional context.

Imagine Martin Luther King at the Washington Memorial that day, his words magically projected onto the Washington Monument for all to read:

---

1. HAVE A DREAM

- a. Better Life
- b. Racial Equality
- c. Can See Promised Land

This brings us to a final, seemingly compelling point. Would Lincoln at Gettysburg, Ronald Reagan at the Berlin Wall, or any other great presenters in history have fared better if only they had used visual aids?

Would the State of the Union addresses have more impact if our presidents incorporated PowerPoint?

Are our words made more powerful by slides that lack heart and soul?

Then why do we use them?

Have a very, very, very good reason for using "visual aids."

How to Know You Gave a Terrific Presentation

"I wish she'd spoken longer."

Leave a group wanting to hear more and you have sold something: a second audience with them.

Every day, hundreds of presenters have their listeners in their hands. But they try to cling too long, milk a few more laughs, bask a few minutes longer in the spotlight.

And the audience works their way right back out.

Resist this and people will remember you well, and will want to hear you—no, long to hear you—again.

Don't just make it brief. Make it a little briefer.

FROM ROBIN WILLIAMS TO DR. JEKYLL: RELATING

The Lesson in the
Democrats' Folly

George McGovern, Michael Dukakis, Al Gore, John Kerry.

Each man had done his homework, projected considerable intelligence, and tried to demonstrate a superior command of information.

Voters rejected all four.

The powers in the Democratic Party consistently act as if the race for the presidency is a form of the SAT. Find the person who at least appears smartest: the candidate who can recite policy and its supporting data, and display the best recall of economic policies of the past fifty years. The Democrats think that life is like college, and that the best student deserves the Big Job.

(The older Democrats apparently have forgotten, and the younger ones never knew, Adlai Stevenson. Many voters noticed that Stevenson was brainy, and considered it a weakness, dubbing him "the Egghead.")

The Republicans view people differently. They think that people do not buy superior intelligence and a fingertip mastery of relevant facts. They think voters buy people they like.

So the Democrats keep choosing valedictorians and scholars, while the Republicans pick prom kings—a group among whom Ronald Reagan was a classic representative. Pundits labeled him "The Great Communicator." The Democrats said that of him, too, but with contempt. "He's a communicator, not a thinker," they said, and headed off to find their next Really Bright Guy.

On one recent occasion, the Democrats got lucky. They chose a provably bright man—the Rhodes Scholarship committee screens very tightly for that quality, as everyone knows. But Bill Clinton also knew what the Republicans knew.

Like all buyers, voters want someone with whom they can relate. So Clinton tried, and succeeded; he talked about everyday people and everyday problems, in an everyday slight Arkansas twang. He stands alone as the only Democratic candidate in decades who would think of uttering the expression "I feel your pain."

Why do people choose you and not someone else? Is it for your mastery? Or is it because something in you resonates with them?

We choose emotionally resonant people because we prefer their company—even if it is only via televised presidential press conferences. We choose people for their spirits, because even the very detached among us have souls, and it is there that we live.

We buy how good you are. But assuming you are among several candidates whom we consider capable, we buy not how good you are at what you do.

We buy how good you are at who you are.

Cultivate your mastery, but cultivate the rest of you.

Every Sale Is Emotional

We evolved emotionally first, and still are emotional, subrational, intuitive, and instinctive. To put it quite simply, as something we routinely ignore, we are animals.

We are so animal, in fact, that we share 98 percent of our genes—forty-nine of every fifty—with chimpanzees. We are, as Desmond Morris memo-rably wrote, *The Naked Ape*.

This means that if all you give people is reasons to hire you, buy your services, or give to your cause, you will appeal only to a small part of their mind. To twist the words of the old song, the head bone connects to the heart bone. Emotions do not operate separately from reasoning; they often dom-inate them. Emotions change thinking; researchers can demonstrate that to you on a brain scan.

We think with our entire bodies and beings.

You must appeal to all of that, too.

Reach the head through the heart.

What People
Crave Most from You

Our primary needs are for food, shelter, and clothing. But most people already have fulfilled these needs. They have replaced these needs with desires, of which their greatest is to feel appreciated.

Following appreciation, we desire—and demand, as you can see sculpted in highest relief in the movie *The Godfather*—respect. You see this passionate desire expressed in the rages of our age: road rage, register rage, airline rage.

In each case, the rage is triggered when someone acts disrespectfully. "How dare you?" is the obvious thinking when Don Corleone orders a hit, or when a driver blares his horn at someone who cuts him off in traffic. It's not "How dare you?" we think in those cases.

It's "How dare you *do this to me?*"

Our desire for respect leads to another demand of our age: the need for manners. It seems unnecessary and painful to chronicle the evidence of the decline in civility. Twenty years ago in most American cities, drivers needed to see green lights to know when to hit their accelerators.

Today, they needn't worry. If they delay even slightly, the drivers behind them will signal Go: they will blow their horns.

Thirty years from now we will see movies with loud horns, even louder stereos blaring from open car windows, and loud voices over cell phones, and know the movie is set somewhere around

2007. But like all epidemics, this represents a problem and an opportunity.

The person who understands manners will be treated well—and regarded highly, and the fundamental desire to which you must appeal is the strongest desire you have: the desire to be treated as important.

Honor each person's craving to feel important.

The Key Moment in Every Relationship

It's the very first.

Surveys of service firms regularly show that the act that most influences people's satisfaction is the welcome. In one survey, 96 percent of the clients who said that they felt "very welcome" when they entered the company's office, said they were "very satisfied" with their overall experience.

Welcomes not only begin a relationship well, but frame the entire experience. The recipient feels more engaged, which in turn, engages the provider in a virtuous cycle.

Master your welcome: the way you greet others, the way you answer your phone. Check your e-mail autoresponse, too, because it frequently acts as your greeter. Does it sound welcoming, too?

Master the welcome.

All We Need Is Love

Just as colleges insist that teachers write regularly—that they "publish or perish"—William Zinsser once observed that the best learning does not come when you read, but when you write.

As you write, you write not only about what you know. You write what you figure out as you write. The act prompts your mind to make connections, and those connections become a thread of thought.

Speaking also enlarges your understanding like few other experiences. It's not easy for anyone, and the thought of speaking terrifies millions. But every time you speak, you learn.

A vivid example was a March 1997 speech on the Upper East Side of New York City, at a presentation hosted by the Learning Annex.

The speaker focused on the emotional drivers behind people's buying decisions. At that moment of his talk, fear was a favorite topic. Fear explained, for example, why a young couple traveling from Tampa to Orlando to visit Disney World would stop at a familiar restaurant like Burger King rather than a less familiar one with better food and service. Fearing a bad experience at the less familiar restaurant, they choose a less-than-ordinary one at a typical fast-food stop.

At the end of the presentation, a woman raised her hand with a question. "You talk about fear, insecurity, the desire for comfort, and other emotions," she said.

"But what about love?"

The presenter immediately learned something. He learned that when a speaker answers, "That's an intriguing question," it means, "I have no idea how to answer, but maybe I can stall for time."

No sooner had he bought that time, however, than the answer came.

"My work is the clients that I love," he said. "Everything else is just cash flow."

That wasn't the key insight, however—as important as it was to realize that work is personal, and that relationships are among the greatest rewards. The key insight, for years that followed, was his understanding of the remarkable role of love in work.

Love: we want to feel loved. It's true of all of us. It's even true in someone who, from his background, would presumably fall among the last people who would ever use the word "love" to describe what he needs at work: an engineer.

This particular engineer was describing an event common to clients: those frequent days when his service provider's representative was "in the area." The engineer spoke for hundreds of clients when he described that experience.

"I want to think I am your only client," he put it memorably. "So when you are in my area and you visit someone else, I want you to at least stop by and say hello."

He went even further. He added, "I'm not thrilled you have other clients. I want to be your only one."

The language of love, is it not? A love song includes that very lyric: "I want to be your one and only."

We want to feel important, even loved. The slightest of slights can trouble us.

We want to feel loved, no matter how well we hide it.

The Importance of Importance

There are big egos.

But there are no invulnerable egos.

All people are fragile.

Everyone's ego is pocked with Achilles' heels. Consider, for example, one of the most successful and seemingly indomitable women of the past fifty years: *Washington Post* publisher Katharine Graham.

During her tenure with the *Post,* it became one of the world's most esteemed newspapers. It won Pulitzers, changed the world, and made billions of dollars, much of which went to Mrs. Graham.

By the end of her tenure, Graham enjoyed wealth, fame, power, and the solicitude of millions. She had fans and fawners, lovers and passionate friends.

Yet she remained like all of us: prone to injury from the tiniest fall. She confessed to it.

For all the attention that she received, Mrs. Graham could not abide the slight she felt every time someone—for innocent reason—misspelled Katharine. (Google her today, and you will see this mistake repeated many times.)

"How could these people not take the time to find out how to spell my name?" she asked herself. It's a reasonable surmise that Katharine never forgot the mistake, or the person who made it.

Whatever they tried to sell her, even if it was only a point of view, they failed.

They did not take the time for her. They did not care enough, she felt, for her.

Despite being among the most important people in the world, the slight made Mrs. Graham feel unimportant.

College football history might be different if Ohio State football coach John Cooper had known "the Katharine Graham Lesson." In 1999 he learned about a high school senior who, playing just his first year of football, had quarterbacked Findlay High to the second round of the Ohio

State playoffs. Cooper went out to meet the young quarterback and encouraged him to attend Ohio State. The young man might have, but he decided the coach could not have been that interested: Coach Cooper repeatedly called him "Rothberger."

His name was Ben Roethlisberger, who in only his second pro season led the Pittsburgh Steelers to victory in Super Bowl XL.

Make the person feel important.

What Do People Want?

Interview clients of personal service firms, and ask, "Why do you continue to work with the person and the firm?"

You assume you know their answer. It's *skill*. People like to work with skilled people.

Judging from advertising, prospects must love skill. Time and again, ads and brochures stress the company's "commitment to excellence." Surely, clients seek the most skilled firms, and retain them as long as they demonstrate their talent.

But they don't. That is not the reason most clients continue to work with services, nor is it the reason they continue to work with you. Skill is their minimum requirement, and they assume many people can meet it.

Instead, their answer is one word. You hear this word from clients more than all their other words combined.

The word is *comfort*.

Hearing this answer dismays the people in these firms. They want to believe, and often do, that they are the best. But overwhelming evidence shows that clients do not choose the "best" firm. If they did, one firm in every industry would own a monopoly.

Among other reasons, clients never feel convinced, even after long study, that they have all the information they need to decide who might be best. They have heard some firms referred to as leaders, for example, but a smattering of colleagues and friends have made them question that. They have not even interviewed all the possible contenders for the title of "best."

They cannot conclusively decide who is the

best. That's the same problem you face almost every week.

You never feel certain which is the best coffee machine, life insurance provider, dry cleaner, veterinarian, or CPA, or the best thousands of choices you make in your lifetime.

You do not make the best choice. You do not maximize, as experts on decision-making insist. Instead, you "satisfice." You choose what makes you feel good. Or to repeat it again, you make the *comfortable* choice. Almost everyone with whom you come in contact makes that choice, too.

Consider the words you use when you make such a choice. How do you explain your choices?

You do not. Your words are not words of reasoning; they are emotional.

"It just felt right."

For that reason, it's worth resisting the advice "First, qualify the lead," or "Identify their hot buttons," or any number of other recommended first things. Instead, before you do anything else, make the other person comfortable. (A variety of steps discussed in the following sections can help you.)

If making the person comfortable isn't the first thing you do, the first thing you do likely will be the last.

A relationship starts with comfort.

The Race Goes
to the Fast

A dozen years ago an association of professionals asked a simple question:

"What do clients value most?"

The clients' answers provide another revealing glimpse into what people value in relationships.

When the association commissioned this study of over 300 clients, the organizers assumed several issues would rise to the top. The first was fees. For more than a year, fee disputes had been raging through their industry. To save money, many clients had taken the work in-house. So fees almost certainly would appear among the top three reasons why the clients continued to work with their current firm.

No: fees ranked ninth.

Being professionals, with advanced degrees and official certifications, the association's members were convinced that technical skills might rank even higher. After all, these people had consistently hired the top graduates, the students who demonstrated the most technical aptitude.

Technical skill surely ranked no lower than second.

Technical skill ranked *eighth*.

What ranked first?

"The individual's demonstrated interest in developing a long-term relationship with me and my company."

But perhaps most interesting of all was what ranked second:

"The speed with which they return my phone calls."

No one expected the response, nor could explain it. Fortunately, no one needed to try to explain it. The people surveyed answered this question.

In the follow-up, interviewers asked the people who had placed "speed of response" atop their list, "Does the person need to answer your question when she returns your call?"

The subjects answered "No." Their follow-up comments finally unlocked the mystery—and the emotion behind these unexpected responses.

It turned out that all the callers wanted was for the professional to call back promptly. The callers didn't expect the problem to be solved immediately, and did not assume their questions could be answered quickly. The callers only wanted what almost everyone wants every day.

They wanted to feel important to the other person.

People yearn for a quick response because of what it conveys: "You are important to me."

Many people realize this, at least subconsciously. Their recorded phone message provides that clue by their choice of words. "*Your call is important to me*, so please leave your message . . ."

The people with whom you are dealing, like you, endure beatings every day. They are brushed off by "service people," kept waiting in lines at airports and government offices, put on hold.

In a world filled with indifference, any gesture that tells someone "you are important" appears to that person as a gift.

Reply quickly. Do everything fast.

Everything You Need to Know About Integrity

"Always do right. This will gratify some people and astonish the rest."

—Mark Twain

The Other Knowledge That Matters Most

A start-up law firm went from being the dream of its founders to the dream job of its region's top law school graduates in less than fifteen years, largely because of its unique promise.

From its inception, Greene Espel assured prospective clients that it would not try to solve every caller's legal problem. "We specialize in seven areas," the firm announced in its ads and brochures. "If your problem falls outside those areas, we will help you find the best lawyer or firm for that issue."

Fifteen years later, you can walk in downtown Minneapolis and randomly encounter people familiar with the legal industry. Mention this particular firm, and a startling number of people will tell you:

"Oh yes. They're the firm that will find people the right firm if they aren't the one."

No one can master everything. No person, product, or service—including yours—possibly can be for everyone. Position yourself as the solution to almost everything, and everyone will see you as the solution for nothing. People want specialists.

But you can, as that law firm does, offer something valuable in this age of so many choices, so many people, and so many possible solutions.

You can be a *source*.

You can be seen as someone who can solve the problem—*or find someone who can*. You can be the person who has just what they need, or who knows who does.

Study your industry and those industries that are closely related. Learn the names of the experts, specialists, and opinion leaders.

Great service providers are complete. Like the law firm, *they know how and know who.* They can help you, or they know who can.

Know how and who.

How to Lay an Egg

A woman has been invited to speak about speaking.

Let's stop right there. You and she already know the dynamics involved in this presentation. The woman must be known as someone who can speak knowledgeably about speaking; to have been invited, she has to have spoken for years, and well. Because of that, she has made a good living, perhaps an exceptional one.

You know that, she knows that, everyone in the audience knows that. That's why they are sitting there.

They want to learn *how* she's done it.

How is she going to win this audience? To win any audience, from one person to one thousand, you must first establish an *affinity* with them. You must find common ground.

You walk into the office of someone you want to persuade. You see a book on his shelf about the Northwest Indians. You mention it, and your passion for the famous speech by Chief Joseph of the Nez Percé and his unforgettable final words, "From where I stand now I will fight no more forever." Your passion is genuine, and so is the affinity that you build in finding this common bond.

You also establish common ground by standing on common ground. You may be speaking from a raised podium. But if you insist on maintaining that distance, that distance between you will remain throughout the presentation—and for years after.

What did the speaker do? Instead of shrinking the distance, she added to it.

"My accountant told me yesterday that I can retire now; it was such good news." What she was saying is, "I've made a lot of money doing this, so listen carefully."

Or perhaps she was actually saying, "I've made a lot of money. Aren't I special?"

She wasn't talking about the audience; she was applauding herself. And her message was unnecessary; the audience members knew she'd succeeded. That's why they were there.

But they didn't want to hear how good she was. They wanted to hear how good *they* might become by listening to her advice.

They didn't want to be reminded how successful she was. That only reminded them that, somehow, they had fallen short.

People don't want to hear how good you are. *People want to hear how good they can be, and how you can help.*

Get on to common ground, and praise others, not yourself.

Common Ground

Ask a group of salespeople, "Have you ever heard of a former Marine making a call on another Marine, and not closing the deal?"'

They all shake their heads.

Nor have they ever heard of a single Notre Dame or Delta Gamma alum calling on a fellow alum or sorority sister, and not establishing a successful relationship.

To strike a deal, first find common ground. Breast cancer survivors know this; they deal with each other in preference to others who do not share their common ground. So do natives of Montana living in the East, Greeks living in America, and more; this list spans pages.

We feel comfort—the key to a successful relationship—with those most like us. Studies of animals other than humans show the same thing; likes constantly attract, while those that are different are shunned. Birds of a feather do flock together—and peck at birds whose feathers look different.

We feel we know people who are similar to us because we know something of ourselves. We feel that we can predict their behavior and reactions because we can predict our own.

This makes us comfortable.

Because first impressions deeply influence everything that follows—more than most of us realize—you must find common ground quickly. Try to find it before you actually meet.

Do your homework. Know the person before

they get to know you. Pay careful attention to places of birth (they are basic to almost all of us), colleges, and hobbies.

If you come to their office, study it quickly: the books on their bookshelves reveal several clues. Their memorabilia often contain even better ones: trophies, photos of fishing or skiing trips, five-year-old's art taped to the walls, symbols of favorite sports.

What if the person's office contains none of this? In that case, realize that you are dealing with someone who is nothing but business. Your common ground can be your passion for your work. Knowing that can be useful, too.

Before you meet, and in the first seconds after you do, find common ground.

Adapting and Adopting

Every day, a million people flunk their sales test without ever receiving a grade. In fact, they feel certain they have performed well: they've been enthusiastic, convincing, and persuasive.

In short, they think just like the woman who made her pitch over breakfast at an Atlanta hotel.

She *was* energetic and animated. *That* was her problem.

Her prospect—she was trying to coax the man across the breakfast table to serve on her board of directors—operated differently. He worked slowly and more analytically. He valued passion, but most of all, his perspective of any business was that of a good investor. He wanted to know, "What difference do you make?"

The woman's mistake was not that she failed to answer that question. It was in *how* she tried to answer.

She answered fast, at near Robin Williams pace. The prospective board member had conveyed to her that he operated more deliberately. He needed information at his pace.

But she missed the signal and forged on, at 120 words a minute.

She failed to do what great salespeople do. She failed to "mirror and mimic."

Every prospect lives and processes information at a particular tempo. Some are waltz, others are rap; some are *adagio*, others *presto*.

To comfort your prospects, they must feel similar to you—and an early signal of similarity is tempo. If your prospect travels at thirty-five miles per hour, you must slow down to mimic his pace. If you choose a faster or slower pace, he senses you are not relating to him or understanding him. Indeed, it appears you are not even trying.

The difference becomes so great, in fact, that he tunes out.

You've failed to adapt to him. By doing that, you have communicated that you are different from him—too different, he decides.

People choose what is familiar to them. A familiar pace—their own—comforts them.

To establish common ground, mimic your listener's pace.

Relating's Magic Words

"Thanks."
　"Welcome."
　The person's name.
　The fourth? The names of the person's children.
　The next four magical words?
　"I'll get the check."

Use the magic words.

What P&G Knows: Five Minutes Early

It's good advice to listen to prospects and clients, but ordinary listening will only produce ordinary results.

Instead, you must listen as if your career depends on it.

The value of intense listening was revealed at an unusual gathering in Lake Las Vegas, Nevada, in the spring of 2005. One of the world's premier engineering consulting firms had invited five of its Nevada-based clients onto the stage, to learn what clients value most from their consultants.

During the one-hour round table, the clients shined a bright light on what people value in the people they hire. No comment was more telling than Doug's.

Like all clients, Doug wanted to feel important to the firm and the individuals he hired. In conveying that desire, he offered that it was vital to him that the consultants "walk in his shoes." He offered good advice: learn not just what he wanted, but how he worked. Learn the pressures and demands of his job.

To learn that, he mentioned that he wanted the consultants to attend his board meetings. Most of the people in the audience heard that and, being conscientious, wrote down Doug's advice: *Attend more client meetings.*

But that isn't precisely what Doug said. He said something more, and more important: he added a word.

The word was "promptly."

On examination, it's easy to conclude that arriving on time for a Nevada Water Board meeting will not add to your understanding of the board's issues. Those meetings tend to start late because at least one key member gets delayed. Like most meetings, the board's begins by exchanging pleasantries, discussing the weather (very important to people in the water industry), and reviewing the games played the night before. The obsessively efficient person, in fact, shows up for meetings in most parts of the country five minutes late, for just that reason; few meetings start on time.

So why does Doug, and virtually every other client in the world, want his consultants to show up promptly? It isn't to make that consultant better informed. Instead, it's what the consultant's prompt arrival communicates: *this is the most important thing for me at this moment*. There wasn't something else—equally or more important—that required my attention.

Ninety percent of success *is* just showing up: *On time.*

To a client, it says, "You are important to me." Procter & Gamble teaches this religiously, in fact. They teach the P&G rule: If you're not five minutes early, you're five minutes late.

Always, on time.

The Extraordinary Power
of the Ordinary

It bears repeating, for several reasons.

Ninety percent of anything is showing up.

When you hear those words at age twenty, they sound comical. You do not take it seriously. You do the opposite. You laugh.

Nearing thirty, you may cling to the belief that success is the residue of mastery. Master your skill, whatever it is, and the world will flock to you. You don't just show up; you show up brilliantly.

Eventually, however, you come to realize that the humor in that joke lies not in how far it lies from the truth. It's how close.

Showing up really, really matters.

You can learn that from helping companies market their services. Over time, a pattern emerges. You see that companies occupy niches in a market, and learn that there are only a few true positions of power.

In services of many—and you are a service of one—one position emerges with special strength and a strong appeal to a large percentage of prospects. We call it "The Reliable Performer."

You immediately can identify some famous businesses that occupy this niche. You may have thought of Maytag washing machines again, thanks to their clever and repeated-for-decades use of their icon, the Maytag repairman. He has nothing to do, of course, because Maytags rarely need repairs.

In cars, the Reliable Performer niche figures so prominently that when the Powers Survey releases its finding on automobile reliability, newspapers devote long stories and prominent positions in their papers to the findings. The survey ranks cars on defects per thousand, and is considered the most reliable indicator of quality in cars. Toyota performs well in these surveys, year after year, and occupies the Reliable Performer niche in the mid-market and mass-market automobile segments. From this reputation, Toyota enjoys massive appeal and excellent annual sales.

Time and again, prospects choose the Reliable Performer: the one that shows up and performs well, but never spectacularly, day after day.

Above all, people choose the reliable. Be there.

The Ordinary
in Action

A very successful management supervisor in a prominent consulting firm, after years of observation, had discovered what he believed to be the five keys to a consultant's success. As surprising as this may seem, the first two were "Show up on time," and "Make sure you have everything you need for the meeting."

He was asked, "How can those two things possibly make a difference?" He answered, "Because other consultants fail at these tasks every day." He cited a recent example—again, these things really happened. A consultant for a competitor showed up on time for the meeting and had everything he needed—except one thing.

He forgot his pen.

No big thing, he decided, and asked to borrow one. Three months later, his former clients still tell the story with a mix of amazement and amusement.

As with large services, so with yours, your Service of One. You emerge from school convinced

that mastering your craft will bring you success. It
certainly can. But the history of business is filled
with stories of those who soared at their best, but
could not maintain that height consistently.

Do the big stuff, but *master* the small. People
look at the small as telling evidence of your ability
to do the big—and anything else.

Above all, perform consistently and reliably.
Ninety percent of success, it turns out, *really* is in
showing up.

Dot the i's. Not everyone does.

Jekyll, Not Hyde:
Being Predictable

Sometimes you pay handsomely for valuable advice. Other times, if you are lucky, you can steal
it on a plane.

Seated by the window on a United Airlines
flight, the traveler hears a voice that conveys un-

usual authority. Attracted to that, the traveler eavesdrops.

The voice belongs to a man who tells the woman he specializes in helping companies communicate to their employees. It is apparent from his comments that he is a fanatical and articulate student of human relationships. By her questions, you learn that the woman has actively studied human relationships, too.

She asks him, "From your work, what do you consider *the* key to successful relationships?"

His answer startles the eavesdropper. Surely he cannot be right, although his background and conviction suggest that he must be.

"Predictability," he answers. "We are most comfortable with people whose behavior we can predict."

Consider his answer for several seconds and its pieces come together. He does not mean predictable as in "repetitive, without variety, boring." He means that people feel most comfortable with people who behave in consistent, and therefore predictable, ways.

You see our fear of the opposite captured, like so many human fears, in a famous story: *Dr. Jekyll and Mr. Hyde*. Doctor one moment and monster the next, Jekyll/Hyde embodies the extreme and classic model of what people fear: the unpredictable.

You know this from your own strained relationships with people with addictive personalities. The addicted person makes you uncomfortable. But you are not uncomfortable with who they are at their worst, or who they are at their best. Instead, you withdraw from them because you are never certain *who* they may be next.

They act unpredictably; that makes you uncomfortable. And comfort is critical to a successful relationship.

The addict represents only the extreme example of a person who discomforts us. The person who responds to a call immediately one day and the next one three days later is another.

So is the merchant who posts opening hours at 9.00 A.M., but sometimes comes in at 10:00. Not trusting when he may be open, you start going to another retailer instead.

Are you predictable?

Be consistent: hours, habits, behaviors.

Look Out for the Bulldozer Drivers

The young architect's résumé promised that he would become a star.

His professors raved about his skills. At a time when his industry was suffering a recession, seven firms invited him to interview. He chose one, and began his upward climb. The climb lasted only a few months.

No one told him about the bulldozer drivers.

You learn about the importance of bulldozer drivers from listening to Bill Coore, a growing legend as a golf course architect. When asked how to thrive in his field, he answers, "Get to know the bulldozer drivers. Win them, earn their trust, and persuade them of your vision, and work suddenly becomes much easier."

In this young man's firm, which designed huge office buildings, the "bulldozer drivers" were known as the "support staff," a term that seems to equate people with walking canes.

The term "support staff" misled the young man. He assumed these walking canes were there for him, and with good reason, he thought, given his accomplishments and apparent future.

And then they weren't there to support him. The reason is not hard to figure out. He thought they were canes. They thought he thought that, too.

They won. The young architect was impossible, disorganized, discourteous, aloof, temperamental—they told the partners. Their list went on, some of it accurate, some of it the inevitable distortions that occur when relationships erode.

In the firm, the secretaries drove the bulldozers. They were valuable on a daily basis and indispensable on those occasions, for example, when the architect realized that the blueprint that was due Friday was actually due in three hours. How do you get the blueprint to the client?

You do it only if a bulldozer driver is willing to skip lunch and help you plow on.

You are surrounded by bulldozer drivers everywhere, wearing disguises that might cause you to miss them. The person you meet on the airplane, for example. He drives bulldozers for a prospect, but has the ear of the principals. Make a strong impression and you soon could be making a sales call.

There's an old phrase, used in a different context, that conveys some excellent advice. "You need all the help you can get." *All of us* can use all the help we can get.

Look out for the bulldozer drivers.

The Power of Sacrifice

The study of human relationships shows that one thing binds people together: sacrifices.

In failing relationships, one or often both parties feel the sacrifices are out of balance. One or both feel they are giving more than they are receiving. In successful relationships, the sacrifices feel, and more often are, close to equal.

The first reason to sacrifice is for the sake of your relationships. Your sacrifices create a bond, and these bonds are key to a rewarding life.

But we easily overlook the second reason to sacrifice, especially if we fear that giving to others takes from us. Sacrifices take time and often money; we worry that time and money lost are lost forever.

Yet when we observe giving, experts see something different. Giving benefits the recipient, of course. But psychologists constantly observe that acts of giving boost the giver's self-regard, and for long periods following the gift.

Give for your own sake. Give because it helps you, and not only eventually, from the person who repays the favor. It benefits you *immediately*.

Helping helps you.

FLYING WIGS, SNAKES, AND DEMONS: ATTITUDE AND BELIEFS

Beliefs Work

Beliefs change everything. To an astonishing degree, you are what you believe, and others perceive you that way, too.

As one example, you tend to experience what you believe you will. We learn this in marketing when we ask a person to taste Brand X, a brand they know and like, and our brand. They decide that they like ours, but like theirs much more. They cannot describe our product, but can describe theirs in some detail, almost all of it flattering.

The problem, as you may have guessed, is that Brand X and our product are the same product, just in different containers.

If we think we will like something, we do, and we will be able to tell you why we strongly prefer it to other things—*including other absolutely identical things.*

We all have heard of the placebo effect, which is what is at work here. But what many of us do not realize is that the placebo effect is not, in most cases, an example of confused thinking. Placebos actually do work; brain scans routinely show that people who take a placebo to reduce pain actually feel less pain. The pain has gone. They are not just imagining.

You are, then, what others believe you to be. And you are to them, in large part, what you believe yourself to be. We consistently have found that the best salespeople are not those who can somehow muster great confidence in the service they are selling. Instead, they are the ones who genuinely believe, utterly and absolutely, that theirs is a superior product. Your belief in yourself will inspire it in others.

Belief works.

Do What You Love

It's axiomatic that if you do what you love, the money will follow. But is it true?

No. The money often follows, but often doesn't. But rule or no rule, it does not matter.

Do what you love anyway.

Doing what you love works.

First, the money may actually follow and please you. Given that we need some money and enjoy having a little more, that can happen.

As one alternative, you may find that money follows but pleases you less than you had expected. That happens regularly.

As the next alternative, the money follows but pleases you only briefly. That is the most common outcome, for a reason that may be inherent in human beings. Abraham Maslow once observed that alone, perhaps, among all animals, humans are capable of only temporary satisfaction. Once something satisfies us, we move on to our next unsatisfied desire.

Satisfaction—as you learn when you study the satisfaction of clients of businesses—typically lasts for only moments. Satisfaction simply raises our bar.

As a final possibility, you may find that the money does not follow, which might disappoint you.

But none of these outcomes matters as much as the guaranteed outcome: *You will have loved what you've been doing.* That will satisfy you so deeply that the result must either be called success, or recognized as something even more enriching.

Do what you love, and the pleasure of doing what you love will follow.

But I've Heard This Before

We assume that if we've heard something, we know it, and if we know it, we are acting upon it.

But people constantly repeat advice because all of us constantly ignore it.

This fact actually is a phenomenon: It's a form of magical thinking. We believe that when we hear something, we learn it, and that once we learn it, we believe we act on it.

We don't.

You find a parallel to this in at least three-fourths of all companies. They have made a plan. Because of this, they believe they are executing the plan.

But knowing is not doing. And knowing and thinking never is enough.

So if you believe you have heard it before, you have. But ask yourself, and then answer with brutal honesty, the question:

Am I acting on that knowledge?

Three Steps
Forward

For years, book jackets have screamed at you. They've promised that the material inside will transform your life dramatically, suddenly, and with little effort.

If you've soured on those claims, as we suspect, you've come to the right book.

Because as every autobiography shows, even the most successful lives are filled with steps backward. One day, you learn a liberating lesson that removes much of the sting from your mistakes:

Your great strides forward follow your long steps back.

Or put another way, your mistakes are gifts, if only you will open them and look inside.

Just stay with it.

Our Misunderstanding

To a degree that dismays some readers, books about sales often are filled with inspiration.

Most people assume this is because salespeople constantly need to be motivated. We imagine ourselves making fifty cold calls a day and having the phone slammed down within seconds on half of them. We conclude that only someone truly motivated could endure that for more than a day.

For years, salespeople reading these books have assumed that, too. Fortunately for the books' many authors, the readers' appetite for motivation always has been hearty enough to keep the authors' families fed.

But the critics, as well as these enthusiastic consumers, have missed something. Inspiration and motivation are not simply what the salesperson needs to sell; they are a large part of what people choose to buy.

Examine your own purchases over your lifetime—products and services—and think of the people who sold them.

Did the sellers know more about their products and services? Were they able to detail all the reasons why theirs was a superior product? In fact, to what extent did they sell you at all?

In retrospect, and with perhaps a few exceptions, didn't you buy from those you liked, and not buy from those you did not?

And what was it you liked? Their command, their intelligence, their persuasiveness? Was it their heads you bought?

Time and again, you bought their hearts and souls. You bought them and their spirit: their enthusiasm and warmth. Without realizing it, you bought their love of life and their love of people. You bought from them because you enjoyed their company. You went back for the same reason.

And you still do.

What does this tell you about motivation and inspiration? It isn't what you need to get up every morning and make all those calls, or to keep going when business is bad. In large part, *it is what you are selling.*

If you are selling yourself, you are selling your spirit.

Life Is What
You Make It?

The sentiment that life is what you make it assumes you control almost everything. You don't. You cannot control a bad boss, the screaming driver in the next lane, or the rain that destroys your season's crop.

You cannot control your life, but you can control your responses. To draw a parallel, the secret to a perfect golf shot is not squeezing the club tighter. Counterintuitively, Gerald McCullagh, one of America's top golf instructors, advises his pupils to "grip the club like a baby bird." A golf ball travels further when you let go.

(Of course, you *can't* let go, but that's for another book.)

If you insist on trying to control things you cannot, you will keep squeezing tighter until something breaks. Focus on the one thing you can control, however, and life can change for you, literally overnight.

Life is not what you make it. It is how you take it.

Make Yourself Uncomfortable

An athlete learns that "you need to burn to grow."

The philosopher Friedrich Nietzsche learned a similar lesson that he expressed in a different language. "That which does not destroy me, makes me stronger."

Others have observed the wisdom of these sentiments, and have translated it as "a crisis is just an opportunity," or a related idea, "a failure is just a success, the details of which have yet to be revealed."

Everywhere you look, pain is the path to pleasure, and discomfort is the road to something richer.

Make yourself uncomfortable. Make the cold call you do not want to make, the confrontation with an employee that you dread.

Seek comfort and you will shrink into the background, and never accomplish what you hope to.

The first rule: Make yourself uncomfortable.

But I Am Uncomfortable

Good.

What does comfort get us?

There's a related idea from the world of ideas and innovation. We routinely say that if an idea doesn't make you at least a little uncomfortable, it's not an idea.

We business writers are guilty of playing into this notion. We write books that tend to reaffirm what you already know and what you believe you already practice. Our books seem to pat you on the back, say Atta Girl, provide comfort food for the head.

You like that. We do, too; we love to hear that we've been right all along. *But.*

We tend to dispense conventional wisdom, and it makes all of us feel good—for a time. But it's easy to realize that conventional wisdom produces conventional results, and we aspire to more. To get to more, we need to take a slightly different path. We need to stretch—a little at first, then a little more.

A little discomfort is a good thing. A lot usually proves to be even better.

Keep going.

Isn't Easy the Whole Idea?

Seven easy steps to financial freedom.

Seven easy days to thinner thighs.

Seven easy moves to lower your golf score.

Funny how we see those headlines every day.

The reason we see them repeatedly is because freedom, thinner thighs, and lower golf scores still elude us. They elude us because these easy steps do not work. They lead us only to the next easy step, and the next.

That is, they do until you reasonably observe that maybe hard steps work better. We think of M. Scott Peck's gem in *The Road Less Traveled*—that a fundamental sign of mental health is one's realization that life is hard.

You can try to live by the opposite creed, and aspire to not just a simple life, but a life in which everything worthwhile comes easily. But nothing worthwhile comes easily.

Half-efforts do not produce half-results. They produce no results. Work—hard work, continuous work—is the only path to results that matter.

Push. If it hurts, good.

Once More

If nothing changes, nothing changes.

Whatever good advice you find here should do more than make you nod. It should encourage you to do something different today, and then the next and the next.

Choose something in here: anything. Then do it.

If something changes, something will change for you.

Choose the Dots,
Not the Lines

The history of computers was changed by an art class.

In a now widely circulated address to Stanford graduates in the spring of 2005, Apple CEO Steve Jobs spoke about "connecting the dots." He explained this by recalling his year studying at Reed College in Portland, Oregon. For months after he arrived, he kept noticing the dozens of beautifully lettered posters promoting everything: seminars, recitals, plays.

He became curious.

Soon, he learned the explanation for the profusion of handsome posters. One of the world's great calligraphers, Lloyd Reynolds, taught at Reed and influenced an entire generation of calligraphers. Beyond curious and now captivated, but with no other reason, Jobs signed up for a calligraphy class.

Fast-forward to today, more than twenty years later. We see the influence of Lloyd Reynolds and that class everywhere in computers, with their emphasis on excellent typography and its nuances—kerning, letter spacing, line spacing, serifs. We saw it first in Apple's early word processing programs but now see it everywhere (except, of course, in memos we receive from the few holdouts who still set everything in their default typeface, Helvetica).

Jobs decided to take an art class, and the computer was changed by it. He could never have seen that ultimate connection. It just came.

He did not know where his class would lead, but he did not ask, "What can this do for me?" He followed his curiosity and passion instead; he chose the dot.

You often cannot see the lines, but you cannot miss the dots. Your dots, like Steve Jobs's, are your interests, even passions. Follow them, and someday they will form a line that connects you to something wonderful.

Choose the dots.

The Problem with Money (Other than Not Having Enough)

Thirty years ago, a friend studied what industries might become hot and decided on the one that would be his life's work. He wanted big money, and this hot industry looked like it would be minting plenty.

There was just one problem. It's clear—indeed, it's been demonstrated—that no amount of money is enough.

This was suggested in a fascinating *Newsweek* article in 1994. A team of journalists set out to discover, Who in America feels truly rich? And just how much money makes one rich?

The first person they interviewed earned $40,000 a year. Was he rich? He said no. How much would be rich? Twice that much, he said. He'd be rich if he could make $80,000 a year.

Thinking that the number $80,000 might be a widely agreed upon measure of wealth, the journalists found a woman who earned exactly that.

Was she rich? She said no. How much would she need to earn to qualify?

Again, the same answer: twice that much.

So they found someone who was earning exactly twice that much, $160,000. They asked the same questions and got the same answers. "No" and "Twice what I'm making."

They continued this approach until they finally quit with a person who was earning over $650,000 and who—as you've guessed—didn't feel rich, either.

You grab the brass ring and realize it is only brass. You reach back for more. You grab it and realize it's less than you expected. Eventually, you may learn to stop reaching.

Why wait until then? Why suffer what befell this friend? At one point, his business was worth $16 million to him. He looked even more miserable then. Not only did $16 million feel like far less than he expected, but he suddenly had far more to lose. Now he was unfulfilled by what he had, yet terrified he might lose it.

This story does get worse. He did lose it. It was a hot industry, but his iron was not in the fire.

Whatever the answer may be for you, it isn't money.

Firing, Being Fired, and Other Joyous Events

A friend once chose a career based on an article in *USA Today*. (This already sounds foolish, doesn't it?)

The article was among those thousands that appear, announcing "The Ten Hot Careers for the Decade" or something similar. In making that choice, he resembled people who choose law because it sounds prestigious, advertising because it sounds chic, or a Silicon Valley firm because its offices "seem so fun."

In these and similar cases, a pattern follows. Reality takes hold. You learn that the job, the company, the title, or perhaps all of them are less than they appeared to be. Your performance, which never was exceptional because the job didn't suit you, declines.

One afternoon, your phone rings. "Could you please come to my office?"

Axed, let go, downsized.

It's among life's ugly moments—or so it seems. But while you are agonizing over the apparent insult of being sacked, you notice a weight lifting. You realize you have stepped away from where you don't belong, and toward a place you do.

One day, maybe many other days, you will have to say, "Please come to my office." Only sadists and bullies enjoy this moment, and few of them read this kind of book. So you will feel bad, and feel that you should.

Never mind. *Do it anyway.* No one benefits when someone is in the wrong place. They are not doing what they do best, and they will always feel empty.

So don't feel you are doing this out of painful necessity that tells you, "Dave must go." Do it for Dave. It's the best awful thing that can happen to him.

What looks like a shove out the door really is a nice push down the road, three steps forward.

It's okay. Maybe even wonderful.

A Business
Classic

Eleven years ago a columnist asked twenty successful and widely read men and women to name the greatest books on business they had read.

One of his subjects ran a bookstore with a carefully selected collection of business books. Everything about the owner radiated "bookworm"—his owlish glasses, high forehead, and pale complexion. It became obvious he'd read hundreds of business books, perhaps every book in his collection.

He seemed the ideal person to ask the question.

The owner began confidently, citing "footnote books"—the serious books heavy with documentation and case studies. He mentioned four of them. Then he stopped.

"But my favorite," he said, "and one I think is indispensable in business, is back here."

He and the interviewer walked past Philosophy and History and arrived at a small rack of books.

The owner reached down and pulled from the shelf his choice.

The Little Engine That Could.

The interviewer snickered. Business seemed different to him then. He was still convinced that processes, data, systems, and techniques drove business success. He later learned those had their places in business, but just places.

So does *The Little Engine That Could.* "Think you can" is good advice, even if it has become so common it sounds ordinary.

A remarkable entertainer overcame great odds to be embraced by Americans at a time when few African-Americans were. He later told the world only his belief allowed him to succeed. In fact, Sammy Davis Jr. lived so intensely by that belief that when he put his life into words, he summarized it with his title:

Yes I Can!

The bookstore owner, Colin Powell, Bill Parcells, Sammy Davis Jr., the author of *Little Engine,* and the lyricist who wrote "High Hopes" about an ant who insisted he could move a rubber tree plant—all of these people offer timeless advice.

If you are lucky, you have enjoyed the benefit one of us treasured: our mother's faith. Hers was the voice that whispered, when hope seemed

gone, *believe*. It's a voice we hope you hear, too—
even if it is only your own.

Believe.

The King of Confidence

Hayward Field often rocked, but this day was
rolling.

It was day two of the United States decathlon
championships at Hayward Field in Eugene, Oregon.
The din from the always enthusiastic Eugene crowds
roared several decibels higher that afternoon.

Bruce Jenner was on pace to set a world record.

Jenner was still catching his breath from the first
event of the day, and sixth of the ten comprising
the decathlon, when he walked within shouting
distance of three spectators in the infield. One of
them couldn't resist shouting to him the question
on every fan's mind:

"Bruce, what are your chances of breaking the record?"

Today those three boys, now men, still remember where Jenner was walking, and the look of total conviction on his face, when he shouted back to them, almost instantly:

"One Hundred PERCENT!"

If, as many sportscasters suggest, there truly is "110 percent" of anything, Jenner conveyed that much confidence. He knew the outcome and could see it. And then, over the next four events, he produced it.

At moments when doubt takes its seat alongside belief in your brain, remember Bruce. He reminds us of one of our great powers:

It always bears repeating: Believe.

The Power of Peter

It is twenty-three years later. Harry has just reunited with a childhood friend who is in Minneapolis on business.

We were catching up on twenty years, and like all younger brothers, he came to the topic of his older brother, Peter. Peter was not merely working in New York, but living like it: well. He owned a house in the trees just off the train line in Connecticut and a list of clients from the covers of *Fortune* and *Forbes*.

Of course, any sibling who achieves more than we do is a fraud: that is widely known. So sibling rivalry does explain the impulse behind my old friend's comment, as he offered to explain Peter's success.

I remember his precise words:

"Do you know what I never would have given a nickel for when I started in business," he said, "but that turns out to be worth millions?"

My immediate reaction was Lladro figurines at one extreme and tongue piercings on the other. Nothing else came to me. He supplied the answer.

"Confidence. Peter oozes confidence."

He didn't need to tell me. I hadn't seen Peter since the early 1970s, but he so embodied assurance that he had become my model for it. I remember the first time I told a cashier, "Hey, just keep the change." I was borrowing the exact words and tone Peter had used when, at the age of thirteen, he obliged a cashier at a county fair back home.

"Peter believes, and his clients act as if they have no choice but to agree with him. He's never merely confident; he's certain."

As yet another athlete proclaimed on the eve of a game in which his team appeared outmatched, you've gotta believe. Every day you see examples of the Colin Powell Principle, presumably words of his creation:

Belief is a force multiplier.

Prospects rarely feel certain. Most buyers suffer from fear and doubt, as the term "buyer's remorse" reminds us. How can buyers not beware?

They can't. Your confidence can comfort them, and your lack of it can deepen their fears.

Yes, "con" comes from confidence. One's confidence can fool people, which only suggests how powerfully it works. And so, yes, you can abuse confidence; we feel no need to warn you against that.

But beware of the power of your lack of confidence, too. If you no longer can summon confidence in what you are offering, consider changing what you are offering, whatever it is.

Remember Peter.

Confidence and Greatness

If a human being is exposed to 10,000 words a day—the actual number may be much higher—then someone who heard Kenneth Clark's words has read or heard over 80 billion words since they heard his.

Of all those 80 billion words, his still stick.

They came thirty-five years ago, on the thirteenth night of a momentous event in television, PBS's final airing of the series *Civilization*. For twelve weeks, beginning with "The Skin of Our Teeth" and ending with "Heroic Materialism," Clark had surveyed the great achievements in art in Western civilization. Surely Clark, at the peak of his powers and after decades of study, had acquired strong convictions about what made people and their cultures thrive.

Perhaps curiously to many, Clark said he was struck by a force that to many people sounds soft. Certainly *it* cannot be the answer, these people insisted. Yet there again you hear Clark's words, echoing the words of other historians who have examined centuries of human behavior.

"This program is filled with great works of genius. You can't dismiss them," he said. "Surely this must give us confidence in ourselves.

"I said at the beginning that it is lack of confidence, more than anything, that kills a civilization. We destroy ourselves by cynicism and disillusion, just as effectively by bombs."

Confidence, Clark insisted, nurtures life itself.

Belief matters; your belief matters. If we recognize that Mr. Clark must have learned from his decades of study, perhaps we should now decide that belief matters more than we once guessed.

Remember Kenneth Clark.

Go Inside

You grow in business when you grow in life. Business and personal growth spring from the same source, and long-term success comes from long-term growth.

It's a jungle in there, we admit. Snakes, demons—wait, *you* go inside. We're staying here.

Okay, we will try. You should, too.

Go inside.

Those Who Laugh

Life gives us one good reason to laugh every chance we get:

No one, after all, gets out of here alive.

There is a term for those who live vitally, with passion and humor: it's élan. It's utterly compelling to others.

The Italians, too, bestow special praise on people who ignore the weight of life's burdens, and live with its lightness. They call that quality *sprezzatura*, which translates not quite perfectly into English as nonchalance. In his famous self-help book of the Renaissance, *The Courtier*, Castiglione contended that *sprezzatura* is the signal trait of successful people—in his case, the person able to win favor of the members of the Royal Court.

Few women, however, feel nonchalant over their baldness. Your first glance in the mirror does not prompt a feeling of *sprezzatura*. Samson felt weakened by the loss of his hair, but Delilah without hers would have felt naked.

Feeling slightly naked one afternoon in April 1995, a bald mother flew with her husband and two boys to Scottsdale, Arizona. Fortunately, the city was hosting a major Senior PGA Tour golf event called the Tradition. Getting out in the sun and seeing her favorite golfers sounded like perfect compensation for four months of chemotherapy and daily looks in the mirror.

Day one of the event shone in classic Arizona style: bright, dry, warm—and windy. The four walked down the course to the third tee and took their places on its right side.

A few minutes later, three of her favorite golfers arrived on the tee: Jack Nicklaus, Raymond Floyd, and Tom Weiskopf.

At the moment they arrived, a huge gust arrived, too, coming right from behind them. Off flew her hat, which she could live with. Unfortunately, it had taken her wig with it, and was tumbling toward the front of the tee, fifteen yards in front of the golfers.

Golf galleries are famously quiet, of course, but golf may never have known silence this complete. Over a thousand men and women stood silent and wide-eyed. The term "mortified" is perfect. With rigor mortis a body goes stiff, and hers did.

The gallery members' bodies apparently had, too. Like witnesses to a car crash, all were gawking but none were moving.

With a deep breath, her body finally relaxed enough. She ducked under the ropes and jogged diagonally toward the front of the tee and her missing hair. When she finally arrived, she reached down, scooped up the hat and her hair, and turned back to the golfers.

Somehow, her words just flew out:

"Gentlemen, the wind is definitely blowing from right to left!"

People said the laughter could be heard all the way back at the clubhouse, over 800 yards away.

It's a vivid reminder that life goes on. Hardships come but hardships go, and nothing makes both the peaks more beautiful or its valleys more bearable than humor.

He and she who laugh, last.

Comparing Yourself
to Others

A waste of time.

When you see someone else, you only see the part of the iceberg above the water. Below it, the person to whom you are comparing yourself resembles all of us: fallible, flawed, perhaps desperately unfulfilled. You are comparing a person you know—yourself—with someone you know only in part: that part they show to the world.

What's more, you cannot be them anyway.

One night on his *Tonight Show*, Johnny Carson interviewed Alex Karras. Karras had starred in football as a lineman for the Detroit Lions. By the time of this interview Karras had starred in movies and established a memorable stage presence: witty and seemingly at delighted ease in front of any camera. Like most of his audience members that night, Carson was impressed.

"How is it, Alex, that you appear so at ease?"

Karras said it was easy. "No one impresses me that much. People are just people," he said. "I've been in a lot of shower rooms and seen a lot of people naked.

"It's hard to see anyone as a god after you've seen them naked in a shower."

Focus on the positive.
When that fails, think of those naked men in showers.

Be Yourself
(There's No Alternative!)

We've heard it. But as with most familiar phrases, understanding its rationale helps encourage us to heed its advice.

Be yourself, but for a simple reason: you have no choice.

You cannot be someone else. You can only pretend. The problem in pretending, however, is that you encounter only two types of people on earth. Those who see past the ruse, and those who do not.

Those who see past it then question the

person's character and integrity, and they with-draw from him. At best they endure the person, but they never accept him, because they cannot. The person has not presented them with an au-thentic person they can accept; the true person, whom they could accept, is hiding behind his cos-tume.

The second group, small if not tiny, fall for the ruse. There's a simple reason: they are foolish—lit-erally, people capable of being fooled. But people who can be fooled once can be fooled repeatedly. They are capricious and unreliable—just the people you want to avoid.

Be yourself. It is easier to remember, for one thing, and works dramatically better.

SEX (FINALLY), AND OTHER IMPORTANT STUFF: TACTICS AND HABITS

The Power of
the Tiny

We assume that people are rational.

It's what leads many young copywriters to devise ads that list all the features and benefits of a product, and then invite readers to "Just compare!"

Our belief that people operate rationally compels us to present rational cases to them. But are people truly rational?

By the year 1989, Brian, a young advertising man, had completed an intensive, five-year immersion in the world of cardiac medicine—specifically, in the world of pacemakers and defibrillators. Brian knew a brady from a tachy, could read an EKG, and knew the full range of problems and solutions from simple single chamber devices to advanced physiological ones. He'd won major awards for campaigns.

On top of that, Brian had a unique credential in his industry: as a former personal injury attorney and son of a family of nurses and doctors, he had been surrounded by medicine and its language most of his life.

One day that October he got a call from Craig, an acquaintance who was acting as an interim marketing director for a leading local cardiac device company. Craig wondered if the young ad man could help them.

Brian's immediate reaction was, "Talk about a sure thing!" He'd worked with Medtronic, Eli Lilly, Boston Scientific. He'd won awards and mastered the language. And he already knew Craig, who seemed to think very well of him.

You already have guessed the ending. Brian didn't get past his first letter to Craig. The obvious question is why, and the answer was in that letter.

In Brian's letter, he'd summarized his biography. It seemed almost too good to be true. Filled with confidence, he rushed the package to this future client.

Then he waited.

After three days had elapsed, he called Craig. Certain that Craig had been dazzled, Brian asked if he'd received the package. He had. And what, Brian asked as he braced for the response—which was certain to mix awe with praise—did Craig think of it?

His first words: "There was a typo in the third to the last line."

That was it. That, and the news that they were considering other candidates instead.

Rationally, how could Craig reject the most qualified candidate within a thousand miles, perhaps more? Because we are not completely rational. If we were, most of us who own American Express cards would switch to Visa. The rational argument for Visa is overwhelming, but we still are not overwhelmed because the emotional argument for American Express—its "prestige"—wins millions of us.

There's a reminder here: *We are not perfectly rational.*

But the more important reminder is about the power of details. With so many options, your prospects cannot easily tell their options apart.

Which leads to a fundamental rule of modern business: *The more similar two options appear, the more important the differences.* People need to justify their decisions. We also tend to conclude too much from too little information, as we see in stereotyping. The tiniest things matter—in fact, today they matter more than ever.

They are not rational, but never mind.

People aren't rational. They choose the tiny over the huge; so sweat the tiny stuff.

Your Greatest Debt

She has come to you. She's your client.

She had paid for your vacations, your favorite CDs, and perhaps far more.

She has tolerated your mistakes (more than you know).

She has risked her money, reputation, peace of mind, and perhaps her stature at work. She even may have risked her entire business.

She has smiled through the worst, laughed through the best, and recommended you to others.

And now you ask, should I call her?

Should I feel any debt?

Should I convey that feeling to her? And if so, how often?

There is no such thing as too grateful or too appreciative.

After all she has been through, you cannot thank her enough. And few of us do.

You hear the phrase "I cannot thank you enough." Once again, it captures a basic truth: *You cannot thank them enough.*

How many thank-you notes did you send last year?
This year, send twice that many.

Thank People Unforgettably

Customer loyalty became a buzzword during the last decade, but while the buzz is loud, we see little evidence for it.

People do not feel loyalty to companies. They feel loyal to people.

If you want special loyalty, you must give special thanks, as another Christine experience shows:

On December 19, 1994, my phone rang. I recognized the voice and instantly felt a stab in my chest. The voice was my doctor's.

"Cancer."

Then four words that sounded worse. "We must operate immediately."

On New Year's Eve, they did. Fortunately, the doctor thought they had operated in time; my prognosis looked good. When I returned home three days later, I entered the kitchen and beheld a remarkable sight: a stack of mail more than eight inches high.

As I sifted through the pile, two letters required my quick attention.

The first was addressed from a major hotel chain. I was lucky, the letter told me, unaware of the irony. I had achieved special status in their frequent guest program. Like other recipients of these customer loyalty programs, I valued these rewards, however meager. Any tiny perk helps soften the bumps of life on the road.

Looking at my bandages and realizing I would not be traveling much in 1995, I wrote back. "Might I defer these benefits until I was able to return to work full-time in 1996?"

Three weeks later, I received a form letter.

> We received your request to extend your frequent guest benefits. While we regret what has happened to you, we also realize that things do happen, and we are unable to defer your benefits.
>
> But we hope to see you soon.

The hotel chain was not alone, however, in receiving my request for a one-year deferment. I sent one that same week to my hometown airline, Northwest Airlines. Their response arrived four weeks later, in a handwritten letter:

> How can we thank you for being one of our best customers? We are happy to defer your

benefits for a year. In addition, we have enclosed four complimentary airline tickets to take you and your family away from the cold Minnesota winter and give you a break from your treatments.

Thank you, Christine, for your business. We will miss you this year.

Sincerely,

John Dasburg, Chief Executive Officer

Mr. Dasburg did not know me. He did know that as a resident in a city dominated by his airline—over 70 percent of its airport's gates serve Northwest planes—I often had no choice other than his airline. That didn't matter to him, apparently. He rewarded me anyway.

I have rewarded him back every day since. Will I ever fly any other airline? Only if Northwest does not fly to that destination.

Will I tell this story repeatedly for the rest of my life? With passion and appreciation.

John Dasburg thanked me unforgettably. Now and earlier, his airline has reaped the rewards of his loyalty. They have earned mine, and impressed others through my constant retelling of their story.

The hotel chain has fared less well. While I omitted their name here, I always mention them when someone asks about their hotels. I avoid them. I assume they cannot be experts in accommodations, because they seem incapable of accommodating.

A cancer victim made a modest request of them. Their reply essentially told me that they, like life, were unfair.

The hotel's letter reminds all of us: Be careful. Bad deeds rarely go unpunished, and the punishment often exceeds the crime. The hotel chain has lost a dozen clients—and one of its Platinum Members—over a letter that gained it nothing.

And, of course, be a John Dasburg—and thank you, Mr. Dasburg, again and again.

Say thank you unforgettably.

Thanks

Three in four executives consider applicants' thank-you notes in making hiring decisions. Apparently, most people do not realize this. Only one in three applicants thinks to send a thank-you note.

This suggests again the wisdom of simply showing up. It appears that two in three people do not.

Say thank you. You won't be alone, but you still will stand out.

The Selfish Value of "Thank You"

Remember the last time you thanked someone?

How did you feel then and for the few moments that followed?

Content. You felt content because you experienced gratitude. It was your own gratitude, but your gratitude pleases you, too.

We rush along life's road and slam into potholes. You can feel overwhelmed, cheated, dismayed. Then you reach out with a word of thanks, and a tiny miracle occurs: that feeling passes.

Thanks feels good to you, too.

How to Write an Effective Thank-You

Write four sentences, by hand. (Handwritten notes feel like gifts because you took the time to find the paper and envelope, write the note, affix the stamp, and gift-wrap your note in its package.)

Don't sell. You've already done that. If you try to sell, the reader will decide that you aren't actually saying thank you. You are simply using a thank-you as a pretense for making another pitch.

The sales-free thank-you works for a simple reason. Few people possess the sense and courage to write one. They think good people must "always be closing." So they keep closing.

That opens the door for people like you, who know just where to stop.

At "thank you very much."

Keep your selling and your thanking separate.

What Your Cell Phone Says

You are enjoying lunch. Then it happens.

Your companion's cell phone rings.

What is your companion communicating? That any conversation he may have over the phone matters more than the one he is having with you.

You know how that feels. Now you know what not to do the next time you go to lunch.

We don't need to hear your conversation. We'd rather enjoy ours.

Do as the Chinese Do

A visit to Beijing can leave you with the feeling that our futures may be brighter.

Instinctively, it seems, the Chinese understand

mindfulness—the quality of being aware of those around you—and the value of treating those anonymous others as if they are not anonymous at all. (Perhaps it is impossible not to be aware of others in China, given that those "others" number over 1.5 billion people.)

Watch someone in Beijing on a cell phone and notice something you never see in the United States: the person's left hand cupped over his mouth and the phone mouthpiece, so you cannot hear a word.

Because of that, you are enjoying what everyone craves: peace.

Please.

Talking on a Phone

An administrator at a small Missouri college is waging a valiant war for all of us.

Her weapons, which she carries everywhere, are half a dozen plastic bugs.

Whenever someone interrupts her quiet by talking loudly on a cell phone, she reaches into her briefcase, pulls out a critter, walks over to the person, and hands the bug to him.

"What's this for?" the surprised beneficiaries invariably ask, suspecting she is giving them a small gift, or perhaps a promotional item.

"You're bugging me," she replies.

Talking on your cell phone for everyone to hear communicates that you do not care about anyone. What's worse, they know who you are and your business.

How do they know? Because your business card, with your name prominently displayed on it, is hanging from your briefcase beside you.

PS: No matter how quiet we try to be on a phone, it's still too loud.

Keep your phone calls private.

You Never Make Cold Calls

Anyone you call already knows, or think they know, who is calling.

They have limited information about you. From that, they have done what people do repeatedly:

Once again—we cannot say this too often—they have stereotyped you.

The voice you hear, or the person you see, is not coming to you cold. He has an impression.

Before you make that call, ask: What is this person's stereotype of me?

What's the fastest way to overcome that—so dramatically that he will want to listen?

Before you call, send the person a letter that will make him question his fears. If he has positioned you as "creative," for example, he likely fears that you are disorganized, overly independent, and difficult to manage. That's the "creative" stereotype.

Send him a well-organized letter that praises a former boss and mentions how much you benefited from collaborating with others.

To overcome the coldness of the call, overcome the recipient's stereotype.

Comfort and Clothing

It is true that in choosing clothing, your first criterion should be comfort.

The comfort, however, is that of those around you.

To understand this, reflect on one of the surprising discoveries of our work with businesses. For years, we regularly interviewed our client's clients. Among other insights, we wanted to learn what made our client special. So we asked, "Why do you continue to work with our client?"

The answer these men and women uttered more than all other answers combined was a single word:

Comfort.

"I just feel comfortable with them," they said repeatedly.

The first key to success—whether it is winning a job, a contract, or an ally—is to make the other person comfortable. Comfort starts from your first appearance.

Your package provides the cues and clues. In choosing what you wear, your first thought should not be to impress or intrigue. *It should be to put the other person at ease.*

That means you should rule out excess. For men, rings other than wedding rings convey discomforting impressions to many others. Bracelets, even more so. That funky tie you got for your birthday? Forget about it! For women, a simple criterion for what *not* to wear: any dress that inspires a true friend to scan you from head to toe and say, "You go, girl!"

Yes; that's out.

Dress for the other person's comfort.

The Rule of OMT (One Memorable Thing)

A career in marketing provides at least weekly reminders of the power of simplicity, and the role of the unforgettable.

A wardrobe expert learns this, too. If you wear one memorable item of clothing, never pair it with another. A bold tie makes a powerful visual statement; the same tie paired with a bold-patterned shirt mutes both messages and turns a statement into a shout.

The legendary ad man David Ogilvy knew this. He wore conservative coats, shirts, shoes, and ties—and fire engine red suspenders.

The less famous but noteworthy advertising man Lee Lynch knew this, too. Proud of his Irish heritage, Lee's memorable device was anything green—most often a green tie.

A former Catholic nun turned market researcher discovered one memorable thing one day. Learning that her client loved baseball and things that were offbeat or unusual, she ventured into a store and discovered, to her delight, an unusual baseball. Conventional baseballs are made from white cowhide that is stitched around the ball's core with red thread. This baseball's hide was a rich brown, with matching brown stitching.

She bought it, wrapped it nicely, and mailed it to her new client.

It began a lasting professional relationship.

It's repetitive to say that we remember the memorable. But it's worth remembering in an era when so many companies have so many options—in services, products, potential employees, advisors, everything. Like the manufacturer of cornflakes, how do you break through?

Find a memorable visual: red suspenders, green ties, or perhaps a few brown baseballs.

Look for One Memorable Thing.

A Very Good, Very Dark Suit

Every man and woman should own one.

Because you can never go wrong.

You can buy the appropriate combinations of a French cuff shirt, complementary scarf, cuff links, pearls, an excellent pair of black shoes, and wear it on any business trip to America's best-dressed cities, New York and Chicago.

You can wear it with a short-sleeved print shirt or shell, and look just right in America's most casually dressed city, Honolulu.

You can wear it to important evening events and minor business calls and, with the right accessories, look perfect.

Why very good, and therefore relatively expensive? Two reasons: Very good flatters you more. Very good looks successful without appearing flamboyant or extravagant.

Expensive ultimately costs less, because well-made suits last longer. Given how many times you can and should wear that suit, it's cheaper to invest in one that lasts.

One great suit.

Expensive Black Lace-Up Shoes

Every man should own a pair.

Because they never look wrong. (In many places and with most suits, loafers look too casual, as their name implies. They were designed for loafing.)

Because top executives insist on wearing them, and take seriously people who dress like them.

Because they go well with the very good, very
dark suit that you just bought, and look less conspicuous than a beautiful brown pair.

Because well-made shoes last longer.

Because women notice shoes, and you often
are trying to persuade a woman.

Because they look more serious, and you often
want to be taken seriously.

Because they look successful, and you want to
look that, too.

And one pair of great shoes.

Why Impressive Briefcases Work

Because it packages your work, and people judge
books by covers.

Because it says, "My work is important to me."

Because it makes you look more organized, and

90 percent of prospects and employers want someone who is well organized.

One great black briefcase. (PS: The similar goes for plumbers: One expensive and spotless tool case.)

The Principle of Fail-Safing

Film buffs and students of nuclear war recognize this term. The movie *Fail Safe* made it famous. Fail-safe refers to the steps one takes—in this case, preparing for nuclear war—to make yourself safe from failure.

In Betsy Redfern's case, fail-safing manifests itself on any of the many days a year when she and her company, MWH, host an out-of-town client. The guest is slated to arrive at the massive Denver Airport. Frequent travelers immediately identify the possible problems. You get to Denver Airport.

Where is your car? You cannot find it.

Who do you call?

Some hosts would leave their visitor the phone number for the car company. Others, more thorough, leave you their phone number and the car company's. Betsy, however, gives you her number, her office number, her home number, the car company's number, *and* her assistant's home and cell phone numbers. (At this writing, Betsy, MWH's director of learning, is thinking about buying a second cell phone, in case someone calls all the other numbers and fails, and her first cell phone has exhausted its batteries.)

It's impressive to see Betsy in action. But it is more than that. *It is deeply reassuring.* You travel most places in the world under a cloud of high anxiety. Air travel is the world of Murphy's Law, as every traveler knows: if something can go wrong, it will. Repeatedly.

When you fly to Denver to visit Betsy and her company, you sleep the entire flight. When you choose the people with whom you want to work, you choose whomever Betsy works for, because she gives you something that so much of life lacks: predictability.

Back up everything, double-cover everything, always have a contingency plan.

Cleverness

Almost twenty years ago, a young advertising executive appeared at a panel discussion before a group of a hundred people. With studied nonchalance, he pulled from his briefcase and placed on the table in front of him, for all to see, an unusual prop:

What was then called a "mobile phone."

Naturally, he did this to convey his importance. He failed to put himself in the audience and see what they saw: an insecure young man.

An account executive at a leading Manhattan-based advertising agency was in front of the top marketing executives of a Fortune 200 company. The board had invited representatives of three agencies to attend a briefing before their pitches for the company's business. The nature of that meeting suggested just what the hosts wanted: an opportunity to lay the ground rules for the presentations and provide whatever information each agency needed.

This particular executive, however, thought he was clever. He believed he could move his agency into an early lead by impressing the client. At least once every eight minutes, the executive would find the occasion—often at great strain—to mention his agency's previous work for several Fortune 100 clients.

The prospects were not impressed. They were insulted that the executive thought they could be fooled. They felt uneasy with the man, who failed to understand the rules of that engagement: *You are here to listen to us and ask questions.*

The executive was convinced that you can fool people.

Another executive was presenting to BIC Corporation. She had done all her homework. She forgot, however, one important thing:

A BIC pen.

Several minutes into her presentation, she realized her mistake. She tried to hide her Paper Mate, but her effort was too obvious. Compounding the problem of her attempted deception, the missing pen so distracted her that she missed one of the prospect's questions.

Finally she excused herself, left the room, and came back with a BIC pen in hand. She left the room with the BIC pen, too—but without the BIC pen contract.

You can fool some people now and then. The only problem is, the people you can fool are the very people you do not want to do business with.

That's partly because if you can fool them, someone else can, and will, too.

Never try to fool anyone.

A Must to Avoid

An old saw encourages us never to discuss religion or politics.

Don't.

No politics.

And Another

Everyone believes and worships a little differently. But others gravitate to what they find in you that is similar to them. The more you explore your faith, the further away you can appear.

There is no traction here.

Still the rule: no religion.

Don't Say This
Either

You are at a gathering when Sally introduces herself. She's with Acme.

Never ask, "So what does Acme do?"

Acme may be sponsoring the event, and Sally is stunned you don't know, or haven't taken the time to know, what her company does.

Or they're just a decent-sized company, but she still is proud. You've hurt her by knowing nothing about them.

Or she owns the company, and is even prouder and more hurt.

"I hear you are doing great!" Granted, you

haven't heard, and saying that is a risk for another reason: Acme could be down 30 percent for the quarter, which you would know if you'd read the Business Section this week.

Apparently you do not, which marks you as not only deceptive, but out-of-touch.

Stick with, "What is your role there?"

Sex (Finally!)

The *New York Times* ran an article about businesspeople who travel with their spouses, and noted a popular trend:

The spouse, usually male, brings his wife for the first half of a business trip—and his mistress for the second.

The article also noticed what the traveling executives had failed to see. The only thing anyone in their company admired about those executives was their audacity. The comments of others, even the most liberal and forgiving among them, suggest that we may forgive other's flaws but expect them to keep them hidden.

The comments also remind us: People fear that people who break promises of marriage will break other promises, too.

In the bedroom, yes. In the boardroom, no.

More Sex

We recently learned of Emma, who had been ostracized by a former friend and business associate. Her associate said he might continue his friendship with her if, and when, the woman finalized her divorce, or stopped having dinner with other men while her divorce was pending.

Until then, the man simply could not associate with Emma.

This morally upright fellow currently was married to a woman who was married at the time of their first through eighth dates. He felt a special affinity throughout their courtship, perhaps in part because he and his date shared something in common.

He was married, too.

Yet he was deeply offended by Emma's behavior—behavior identical to his own.

Beware. It's not just the prudes you will offend. It's the philanderers, rogues, cheats, and Lotharios.

Politics and religion are deadly subjects; sex is worse.

Sex: Great in theory, lousy in practice.

How to Be Believed

Admit a weakness.

It will disarm some people's resistance.

It will strengthen every claim of strength you make.

Some researchers discovered this years ago, when they learned that small criticisms of a job candidate made a reference's praise of the candidate far more credible and powerful. The people reading the applications were more apt to interview the candidate who had received those gentle critiques.

Admit a weakness.

Secrets

Keep them. Protect them for just what they are: sacred gifts. They are gifts of trust, given to you for safekeeping.

They are bestowed on you because you have earned your confider's trust, the heart of all great relationships. Keep those confidences and your friendships will deepen. Reveal them, and you slowly will watch a remarkable unraveling: a vivid example of a vicious spiral.

You reveal a confidence. Now the person to whom you have revealed it knows the secret and something else:

He knows you are not to be trusted. He has several close friends, and to them he reveals your betrayal. They spread the word further, to others who do the same.

Betrayals spread like viruses.

The words themselves suggest something here. We "confide" in people with whom we feel "confident"; the words share the same origin. But if I cannot confide in you, I cannot develop a lasting relationship, and others will learn this, too.

Keep every secret.

Mistakes

Admit them.

People decide that a person who admits mistakes is honest. They will trust everything else you say.

People decide that a person who never admits mistakes is insecure and cannot be completely trusted.

The heart of a great relationship is trust. Admitting mistakes is among the fastest ways to build it.

Confess.

Do unto Others, if Only for Selfish Reasons

Three young men raced out in quest of riches and fame twenty years ago. None came back.

The three shared, in addition to their shaky friendships with one another, a conviction that hard work combined with cleverness would one day open the vault. One confessed one night that "image is everything," and set out to create one.

Each made big deals along his way. For several years each earned rewards, and their success made their path look appealing to others. The trio also made it appear that life is a zero-sum game: to get you must take. Do this cleverly enough and you don't get caught; you do get rich. Perhaps some of those others followed.

Each ultimately learned something surprising.

Contrary to conventional wisdom, life is fair.

To appreciate how this works, at least in the case of those who think success must come at the other's expense, consider the discovery of a group of psychologists from tests over the last fifteen years.

In these tests, called "Ultimatum Games," two people are assigned to a team. The leaders of the test offer Al $100 and this instruction: You can give as much or as little of this to your teammate, Brandy, as you wish. If Player B accepts your offer, you both get to keep the money. If she refuses your offer, neither of you get anything. You must give the money back.

Logic insists that Brandy, who had nothing before, will be happy with whatever she's offered. If Al wants to keep $80 and give $20 to Brandy, Brandy would be an idiot to refuse. If she does, they forfeit everything. She loses $20.

But losing that $20 is exactly what Brandy regularly decides to do. In fact, in one set of experiments, Al offered Brandy an average of $40. Even then, in one in six cases, Brandy refused.

Because no matter how much we repeat "life isn't fair," we still insist that it should be. Wherever we can control the outcome, we insist on fairness.

We demand fairness. We punish cheaters. We undermine those who we think have bent the rules.

Readers will be encouraged to learn something else from these experiments. In most cases and cultures, Al offers Brandy a fair deal: a 50-50 split. So not only does Brandy tend to demand fairness for herself, but Al tends to offer fairness, too. After years of hearing the Golden Rule, people apparently tend to follow it.

Those three young men thought otherwise. They thought life might work like *The Godfather*, or perhaps how, in their limited and inaccurate view, it worked for Donald Trump. Instead, life worked just like it did in Ultimatum Game experiments. Each reached a plateau, and then fell. No one was waiting to catch them.

Do good unto others, it appears, and they will do good back. Do otherwise, and the three young men remind you what happens.

Always be fair. The rewards come, and the penalties are huge.

How to Make a Great First Impression

The first time you promise something to someone, indicate the precise time you will deliver on your promise.

Then beat that deadline by half a day.

Say P.M., deliver A.M.

About Criticizing

Alice Roosevelt Longworth became notorious for her famous quote that captures the heart of a gossip.

"If you cannot say something nice about someone," she said, "come sit over here by me."

(She also is known for a remark she made the

day after her first child was born, when Alice was forty-one years old: "I'll try anything once.")

What Alice did not become, however, was a friend. Many people avoided her entirely while others never felt comfortable enough to extend their friendship. They were smart. Instinctively, they knew that it is true that those who speak badly of others will speak badly of you.

Dale Carnegie recognized this decades ago. He stressed speaking positively and not critically, because he knew that people are afraid to befriend critics. They fear, based on experience, that a critical person eventually will criticize them.

They're right.

Accentuate the positive.

Flattery Will Get You Nowhere

The phrase above is famous, and true.

Flattery typically fails and often backfires. Flattery is that form of praise that gives itself away.

Many people consider Dale Carnegie to be the Godfather of Business Flattery. His legendary book encouraged flattery, it appeared, which in turn earned him the enmity of dozens of reviewers. Carnegie's advice confirmed for those critics that business was, as many popular movies were revealing, a haven for manipulators straight out of Machiavelli.

But the fact our language features so many ugly synonyms for false flattery—"bootlicking" is a personal favorite—suggests how dimly we view false flattery.

Carnegie actually was coaxing something different from his readers. He was advocating a view of life that focused on the good. Carnegie saw the good in others and focused there. He saw little value in pointing out a man's bad teeth, and seemed to notice them less than he noticed that same man's full head of hair.

We despise false praise and pandering, but we admire praise-givers. We consider them warm, optimistic, generous, and secure.

We court and love praise. When you dispense it, you hand someone a gift.

Praise often; flatter—never.

No More Mister Tough Guy

Fifteen years ago, America's leading business savior was so tough they nicknamed him after a famous character in a horror movie: they called him Chainsaw.

Five years later, what appeared tough was not the man—Sunbeam's CEO Al Dunlap—but the plight of his company. Sunbeam's stock was cratering, and what had been chainsawed were Sunbeam's employees and the company's future.

Phil Purcell, who managed Morgan Stanley at about this time, acted tough, too. He acted so tough that when his company merged with Dean Witter, many dubbed the new duo "Beauty and the Beast." Purcell ran the merged company with the proverbial iron hand, but when people felt his hand, they fled—managers, brokers, traders, and then, most painfully, the company's clients.

We emerged from a major war sixty years ago. For years afterward, we took as our models of leadership the hardened men of those battles. We embraced the slogan "When the going gets tough, the tough get going."

But that war has been fought and won, and the world of business that once followed its lessons is, as we have learned, no longer a battlefield. And to many people, our wars no longer appear heroic.

A new generation is oblivious to that past, and shows no interest in revisiting it. They are not enlistees in a service, but shoppers, looking for a way to lead rewarding lives. If you can help them, fine. If you cannot, they move on.

You can try toughness, but your trial will produce errors. If you want to sell yourself, your vision, your goals, your product, or your employees, ignore war as your model.

Choose peace instead.

The Power Ties are sitting on racks in consignment shops now, collecting dust; it clearly appears that their days have passed.

Beware of playing the role of the tough guy.

Beware the
Bargain Shopper

If cost-sensitive buyers haggled only over price, they might represent good prospects and clients.

Unfortunately, most cost-sensitive buyers haggle over everything. They want it for less, but they want more.

This takes up time. It also taxes your patience, diminishes your joy in your work, and reduces your margins. If you add up all the costs, the costs routinely exceed the benefits.

Beware the Cost Buyer.

The Power of
Your Price

A Scottsdale, Arizona, based financial planner had been earning what he needed, but not what he wanted, and set out in search of answers.

For two years he read sales and marketing books and tried different techniques, but business remained merely good.

One day, inspired by reading that several products and services had leapfrogged their competitors simply by raising their prices, he decided he would do the same. He increased his hourly and average fees 40 percent.

In the first year following that increase, his income increased 65 percent. Today, his annual income has increased almost 150 percent. He has ceased almost all his other sales and marketing activities because he has all the work he can handle.

It worked for Timberland shoes. It worked for American Express. It's worked for several American universities.

Ask for more.

The Power of Your Price, Part Two

Hearing the story above, the spouse of a Canadian interior decorator excitedly related his wife's experience.

For two years, his wife had charged the going rate for better interior decorators in their province: $75 per hour. Business was good but not great.

So she raised her fee to $125 per hour.

As the husband relates it, the effect was immediate. Inquiries increased, from people eager to work with the region's "premier interior decorator."

Her conversion rate improved, too. Once prospects believed that they were dealing with the area's best decorator—the conclusion they surmised from hearing her fee—they were more apt to say, "When can we start?" Sales took up less time.

The fee increase produced another unanticipated consequence. Her more affluent clientele paid faster, more willingly, and without fail. Cash flowed faster. Tracking receivables took up less time, too.

"It was incredible," the husband reports. (She was busy at work back home when he relayed this.) "I'd never have guessed all of this would happen.

"I just wanted her to earn what she was earning before, but to work less."

Prove yourself with your price.

Time

Some people give and others take.

Assess that immediately. Give your time lavishly to people who give, and avoid those who take.

Your time is precious. Devote it to people you value, and who value you in return.

How to Remember Names

You probably have heard Dale Carnegie's famous words—that a person's name sounds to the person like the most beautiful word in their language.

If you are like 95 percent of all readers, however, this knowledge hasn't helped much. You still forget names often. Take comfort: the people who are best at remembering names often fail, too.

Again, a key to improving is to recognize that you think visually rather than verbally. Your mind struggles to remember words, unless they are repeated so often they cannot be forgotten.

We remember best in images.

We learn this in marketing. Repeatedly, test subjects cannot remember the words of a commercial but vividly remember every image. In other tests, subjects cannot remember companies' names but recognize their symbols.

Take advantage of this. Translate the person's name into an image.

Practice which of these approaches work best for you, but each works for some people.

First, imagine that the person is someone you already know by the same name. Stranger Jim becomes your friend Jim Phillips. You then notice the two Jims have similar builds and hairlines, which makes it easier to remember Stranger Jim.

Or imagine the person is someone with a famous name. You cannot visualize Tom, but you can transform that man into "Tom Cruise." Again, notice a physical trait, perhaps full dark hair, that you immediately connect to Tom Cruise.

Finally, see if you can translate the name itself into an image. Stranger Jim can be a "gym." If Stranger Gym looks fit, think of him lifting weights, or simply connect to your thought "He works out in a gym." Tom can be translated into an image of a tomcat, Julie into the jewels around her neck or on her fingers, Harry into his mop of blond hair.

Try these. But whatever you do, don't try to remember the name.

Instead, remember the image.

Then you will remember the name far more often.

Just to make sure, address them by name immediately so you record the name. Then concentrate on repeating their name, because repetition builds memory, too.

Remember in pictures.

There's Hope

"I don't remember names. Can't now, never have. I've stopped trying."

Gary said that three years ago. Does it sound familiar?

Then keep reading.

Like all of us, Gary fell into the trap of insisting, "I am who I am." He was partly right: Gary was who he was at the moment he said that.

But just as he progressed from a tennis player you could not bear watching to one who could compete with three-fourths of his friends, Gary decided that practice might work. He was certain it would not be perfect, and he was right; he is mildly dyslexic.

But Gary kept practicing. He devised another memory tactic, which was to immediately respond after an introduction by saying, "Now *David*, where are you from?" To imprint the name even deeper, he'd say, "You remind me of my friend, *David* Banner," even when the resemblance was slight.

Gary improved.

You are who you are, but you become what

you do. Gary kept doing, and became better.

He noticed a change. "The more a person heard me say their name, the more they engaged me. The more they engaged me, the more engaged I felt. I felt more connected. I could feel the difference.

"Even if remembering their names never helped me sign a contract with them, the relationships still feel much better."

Just practice.

Your Business Card

You often hear about first and last impressions. You rarely hear, however, how few chances you get to make *any* impression.

You greet someone, talk, hand him a business card, and say goodbye.

A greeting, a conversation, a business card: that's it.

What lingers afterward? An increasingly vague

memory of you and the talk—and the business card, the only tangible and visible reminder.

Your business card also provides one of your few chances to communicate what you must: that you are different.

This explains why people in the aluminum business should consider aluminum cards, and similar thinking should drive people in businesses like fiberglass, corrugated boxes, and micro-processors. It's why the head of a swim school should consider transparent aqua cards, and why everyone should consider cards of different dimensions, materials, and messages.

You want to be vivid, memorable, and distinctive.

You've seen gimmicky cards and decided they don't work. You're right; people loathe gimmicks. They associate them with someone trying too hard, too foolishly, to make an impression.

You don't need a gimmick; you need a vivid and authentic statement. Given that it's all the person may have to associate with you, can you afford for it not to be vivid, memorable, and distinctive?

Now, consider another vital point. Few people like to be sold. A conventional "business card" essentially communicates, "I'd like your business." But you need to establish a relationship before you try to make a sale, which leads to an obvious, but important, conclusion.

You need a nonbusiness card.

Among other benefits, nonbusiness cards make distinctive impressions because few people use them. It communicates a personal message: Please call me, not my company. It moves the discussion away from business, which reduces your recipient's resistance.

How do you do it right? Call a well-regarded advertising agency and ask for an art director. Tell her you need a good designer, preferably with experience designing business cards. (Creative people willingly help, in case you're wondering.)

Interview three recommended designers (ask for samples and budgets). If the budget seems extravagant, do two things.

Ask, can I afford not to make a fabulous impression?

Or, go to the best stationery or paper store in your area, and pose the same question. If you live in a city with a school of design, call the school, ask for a teacher of design, and ask the person to recommend a student. The student needs and would love the experience, and will be talented enough to produce a distinctive and effective card.

People will notice.

Holiday Cards

Millions of companies send their clients and valued business associates holiday cards.

That's one reason you shouldn't.

People are besieged with these cards, during a season when they have too little time to read and appreciate them.

They hear from dozens of people, which makes it far less likely they will take a moment to remember you and your message. (A huge percentage of recipients throw the envelopes out, unopened.)

Worse, you will find yourself sending out so many cards, during a season when you are rushed, that you will be tempted to simply write, "Thanks and best wishes."

Imagine what that conveys. "Jane is so rushed that she said the same thing to me she said to everyone." The reader draws what seems an obvious implication:

"I am one of hundreds to Jane. No big thing."

We crave to be treated as important. Unless you can write dozens of thoughtful and personal notes at the end of the year, don't.

Instead, find special occasions throughout the year to write not twenty people, but just one at a time. Choose a time uniquely appropriate to the client. Birthdays are good, but a card that shows you know more about the person works much better. Try the date of their first child's birth, for example, or the day after their alma mater wins a big game.

The most vivid way to show someone that they matter is to take time. You do want them to notice. So don't send expected messages at expected times. Send special, highly personal ones at special times—times that are special to that person alone.

It's not just how you say thanks, but when and how well.

How to Write an Impressive Memo

In every fat memo there is a thin one screaming to get out, and a reader who wishes it could.

Write one page.

If that's impossible, summarize your memo in your first paragraph.

Tell the readers what you will tell them, tell them, specify the proposed next steps, and then *clearly* request a reply.

Above all, abbreviate.

Following Up

Eric did it; everyone does.

Do you know just how often?

Eric had just finished interviewing four candidates for a position in his design firm.

He had chosen the quartet from a list of ten, and now could not easily tell them apart. Each candidate seemed skilled, affable, motivated, and engaging.

In short, Eric found himself in the position of thousands of people in business every day. Whom do I choose?

Who *did* Eric choose?

The candidate who wrote back after the interview first.

So often, and more often than we imagine, that is the difference in the sale. Several years ago, BellSouth discovered that its two telesupport groups calling on large commercial clients were performing differently. One had received generally good reviews from its customers, but the second group's satisfaction scores were 40 percent higher.

What was the difference? The group with the higher rate of satisfaction had a written policy of following up within twenty-four hours after every contact with a client. The other group had no policy, and averaged more than two days for their follow-up calls.

Follow up within a day.

Snatching Victory
from Defeat's Jaws

You win some, you lose too many.

We all feel that. We agonize all day, in fact, and into the next.

At times like these, it helps to remember that the World Series champion only has to win four of seven games—and often manages only that. The greatest hitters fail more often, more than twice as often, as they succeed. Even the greatest soon realize that perfection cannot be attained, but excellence can. Tiger Woods said just that. "I do not seek perfection, because it's unattainable.

"All I strive for is professional excellence."

You enjoy one advantage over these athletes, however. An out is an out, and a stroke lost in golf is lost forever.

But business works differently. You don't get the deal, the job, the audience with the prospect. That only means you did not get it then.

Someone else gets what you are seeking, but then they fail. Indeed, they fail often. Human resource research has shown that only 25 percent of hiring decisions work well; an equal percentage prove to be total failures.

In deal-making the same percentages apply. Business comes, but so often business goes.

Where will you be when it comes again? You made the finals.

So send that person a letter.

"I was disappointed, of course, to learn that you went in a different direction, but am very grateful you took the time to consider me. If anything changes—ever—I hope you will remember the direction to me."

Two months later, call the prospect with a gentle reminder that you always will be interested. Your persistence will impress the prospect, but something else will impress him more. People admire people who lose graciously.

As a wise man once whispered, "Anyone can cope with prosperity. Handling adversity with grace, on the other hand, impresses people—for life."

Wins come and go. If you persist, losses can, too.

Seek Change

This year, over 300 books will appear that show people how to lose weight. By the end of this year, however, reports assure us that more Americans will be overweight than at any time in our country's history.

We assume that diet books dispense useful advice. We assume people read them, and follow them.

So what goes wrong?

Similarly, this year we see hundreds of books that carry the promise of this one: we can help you thrive at work. By December of this year, millions of people will feel they are right where they began in January.

Is the advice flawed? In some cases, perhaps. One of the issues that often arises, however, is the "been there, heard that." People think they have heard the advice before, so it must not be the advice they need. Instead, they decide they need something new.

But advice is no less true or valuable simply because it has been offered before. And the advice appears again and again because it is repeatedly ignored; even advisors routinely fail to follow their advice. (If we followed ours, we would have written a hundred more thank-you notes last year.)

"I know that," we tell ourselves, and we assume that because we have knowledge, we routinely act on it.

We don't.

We read this advice and instead of taking action, we take comfort. We feel comforted in our knowledge that we have followed this advice all along.

We see a perfect parallel in businesses. We need something new and different, they tell us. We look around and realize that they do not need "new and different." They need "old and necessary." They are like the football team that decides what it needs to succeed is more imaginative and unpredictable plays. You look and say, "It appears what you should do first is master blocking and tackling."

So please, do this. Feel free to assume you already know everything you read in this book. But then, make yourself uncomfortable. Assume you are not acting on *any* of this advice. If you are acting on some of it, assume you are not doing enough. Do more.

Read this book, then act differently. Focus on a page a day, an idea per day. Act on it.

Don't seek reassurance. Seek change.

Then keep seeking.

The Message in *Moneyball*

Michael Lewis did not intend *Moneyball* as a horror story.

Few read it that way either—at first. Most amused themselves instead with Lewis's wonderful account of the Oakland Athletics, and its hero/general manager, the perfectly named Billy Beane.

The book combined two old classics, actually, so it was destined to sell thousands of copies: *Rumpelstiltskin* and *David and Goliath*. Beane took some straw—a relatively small operating budget—and spun it into gold. With straw, he built a team that confronted "big market teams" with their $27-million-per-year star players, and slayed them.

Moneyball charms you.

Then it hits you.

You thought the book was about snubbing conventional wisdom and making a lot from very little. Because what Beane saw differently—out of financial necessity—was how erroneously the enterprise of baseball had measured productivity. *For over a century.*

And it should not have happened. For decades, baseball has almost groaned under the weight of more statistical measures of employee performance than any other human activity.

To their credit, baseball managers and general managers ignored these infinitesimal details. But neither managers, general managers, nor fans ever overlooked the most often quoted statistic in baseball.

For decades, everyone considered a player's batting average as the definitive measure of his offensive productivity. A player who hit .300—who averaged three hits of every ten at-bats—ended any debate. The .300 hitters won pennants.

Then an odd group appeared. They called themselves sabermetricians. One of them found the accounts of every major league game of the previous twenty seasons, piled those records into boxes, and disappeared with them into his Boston apartment for months.

When he emerged from that hibernation, Bill James was convinced that everyone had been wrong.

In baseball, James decided, outs are gold. A team can use up only three every inning; when you're done, you're done. A team wants to use as few as possible, at least until it gets some men on the bases and moves them around to score.

But hits weren't the only way to avoid outs.

There were walks. For decades, however, even the shrewdest baseball fans believed that walks did not represent achievements, but failures: the failure of the pitcher to throw the ball across the plate at least three times in seven throws.

But James discovered that walks weren't always, or even often, the result of a pitcher's failures. If they were, walks would be distributed fairly randomly. David, a third baseman who hits .260, should walk as often as José, the left fielder who hits .335.

But James discovered that some players were very adept at drawing walks, while others weren't. David, every week, month, and year, walked more often than José.

And walks mattered, because they didn't use up outs. A player who hit .260 could actually get on base more often than a .300 hitter, using up fewer outs, and thereby helping produce more runs.

No team had ever valued—figuratively or in literal dollars and cents—players who walked. *Moneyball*'s short story is that Beane read James's findings, traded for guys who got on base often, and started winning. A lot.

What does this have to do with you? Everything.

If, after all that time and data, baseball could not figure out who was valuable, how accurate are the measures of performance in your work? How good are you, and how good do you appear to be to others?

You look the part—or perhaps you're too quiet, too loud, too in-between. You seem like a hard worker—or seem too laid-back. You're good with clients, or maybe not.

To be valued for your work, you need to be aware not just of how you are measured, but the impressions you create. Your skill and talent will influence these perceptions, but that's only one influence. Everywhere you look in business, people are seeing people who get a lot of loud hits and deciding they are skilled, and barely noticing the ones who draw a lot of walks.

Some people will undervalue you. Make a plan to set them right.

THE $18 MILLION SANDWICH AND THE DINOSAUR: SUCCESSES AND DELIGHTFUL FAILURES

Searching for
Larry Gatlin

He said no with good reason.

Grammy Award–winning country singer Larry Gatlin has a second passion in life—golf—and that love each year has inspired several hundred people to plead with him to play in their golf tournaments.

My Christine Clifford Celebrity Golf Invitational was one of those events. But when I learned that Larry was coming to Minneapolis to perform in the play *The Civil War,* I immediately thought of Nido Qubein. A year earlier, I had first met Nido at a National Speakers Association event he was hosting. I told him we shared something in common: cancer. His wife, Marianne, and I both had survived it. I asked for his card so that I could send Marianne my books on coping with cancer through humor.

As it turned out, Nido was as resourceful at hosting speaking events as he was at keynoting them. He had persuaded Mr. Gatlin to appear at his event—for free.

I called Nido. Nido called Larry and made the introduction. It worked.

"When Nido says 'Take this call,'" Larry said, "I take the call."

Unfortunately, that didn't mean Larry was ready to take my bait. Larry volunteered his reasons for saying no. As was known publicly, Larry was a recovering alcoholic. He wanted to make up the time he had missed with his family and new baby granddaughter. As the featured performer in the Gatlin Brothers, Larry also had to earn money for his group.

From this information, I had a profile on my prospect—a key to getting past a prospect's refusal: I was confronting an entertainer, golf fanatic, recovering alcoholic, doting father, and financial provider.

"We'll pay you $10,000," I said, knowing Larry's presence would generate far more than $10,000 for our cause.

"Now you're talking," Larry replied.

Our hometown airline Sun Country Airlines already had donated ten airline tickets to use as we wished. I decided to move most of the chips onto the Gatlin square.

"What if we fly your daughter, your son-in-law, your wife, and your new baby granddaughter to Minneapolis—everyone?"

After a long pause and his sudden burst of laughter, I was surprised by his response. "Really? No one has ever offered that before."

Larry asked to meet personally so he could see with whom he was dealing. We agreed to meet for lunch the next day at the Grand Hotel.

I went into overdrive. I thought again about the man I was dealing with, hurried to my car, and headed to my first stop: the host course for my event, the Minikahda Club.

Just weeks before, the loudest noise in golf wasn't Tiger Woods. It was a golf ball. Titleist had introduced the Pro V1, and it immediately became clear this was no ordinary ball. Its buzz was so intense, in fact, that you could not find the balls anywhere. But I knew there had to be some Pro V1s somewhere, and I knew I had a cause that people cared about.

I approached Minikahda's pro, Doug Nelson, with my challenge.

Doug didn't have a single ball. He didn't even know when his next shipment would arrive.

I pleaded. (While no book on selling or personal effectiveness seems to cover begging, it's worth saying here: sometimes it's your only hope.) Certainly there was some box somewhere that we could find. There is always a solution.

Doug surrendered. "I have a private stash. I

hate to part with them—they really are that good—but for you and the event, you got me." He walked back to his office and returned with my golden box.

I bear-hugged Doug and started to hurry back to my car. But then I spotted something near the door to the pro shop: magic. A tiny pair of pink leather golf shoes made for a newborn, placed there as if someone knew I was coming. *Perfect*.

I charged them to my account, oblivious to the cost. Then to the car and the next stop on my whirlwind.

My new thought: recovering alcoholics certainly have to drink something. I'd noticed that many turn to coffee. But here, the key to Larry's possible gift was the key to any gift. It couldn't be obvious or ordinary. My gift had to reflect extra time and thought.

I knew where I could find that: Gloria's Coffee, downtown, and a rare African blend, a Château Lafite-Rothschild of coffees. There, too, I found an equally rare box of imported chocolates.

Back home, I found an extra copy of *Chicken Soup for the Golfer's Soul*, which included a story I had written. I autographed that page for Larry. Then, one final step: a note to the granddaughter to go with her tiny golf shoes.

"May you become as wonderful a golfer as your Granddaddy."

I arrayed the gifts in a mahogany wicker basket, shrink-wrapped the entire package, took a few deep breaths, and hurried to the Grand Hotel for our first face-to-face.

Yes, Larry Gatlin came to our tournament. He performed spectacularly. His team won the event. And his warmth and generosity won the 300 people who attended his concert that night. Cancer research won, too, raising almost $270,000.

A reader can divine their own lessons from this story, but several seem irresistible:

Search constantly for common ground; we relate best to those with whom we share an affinity.

Invest. Travel the extra mile and pay the extra dollar.

When you say please or thank you, say it unforgettably.

The greatest gift you can offer is your time.

The greatest compliment you can pay is: "I understand something deep in your heart."

Every Day with Morrie

The building looks so plain that most never notice it. There's no reason to suspect that what's inside would make you gasp.

It's a building in Anywhere, Minnesota, about a half-hour west of downtown Minneapolis. It's typical of the buildings that dot these half-suburban, half-rural outposts, except for its size: over 120,000 square feet. There's no sign and no architectural flourishes—although when you learn more about the man behind the building, this modesty seems fitting.

That man's name may sound familiar: Morrie. You stop for a moment. The word "cars" pops into your mind: Morrie's Imports, Morrie's Mazda, Morrie's this car, and Morrie's that.

Cars is right. But while the building is nondescript, the cars are anything but: you come upon four stunning 1938 Packard convertibles, so shiny you think they must be coated in salad dressing, and three classic Thunderbird convertibles. You see older classics that not only suggest *The Great Gatsby*, but recall the novel's famous last paragraphs, where St. Paul native F. Scott Fitzgerald memorably refers to beauty "commensurate with one's capacity for wonder."

Awe, indeed. This man adores automobiles.

And the more you probe, the more interesting the man and his love affair become.

When Morrie Wagener greets you in his office at Morrie's Subaru, he greets you as his own secretary. He insists on taking your overcoat and bringing you coffee. He fusses to make sure you have everything you need before you sit down. After forty years, he's finally remodeled his office, but it's still as modest as Morrie. The furniture is from Office Depot. The gas fireplace between the two windows that overlook I-394 is the only feature that makes this space different from the offices of a thousand young VPs along this stretch of Minnesota freeway.

"Maybe the Dutch really are frugal," he says, a reference to his mother, "and I'm much more my Mom than my Dad." His father was a German-born implement dealer who eventually became a state senator for Scott and Carver counties. And while Morrie's frugality may be classically Dutch, his upbringing had all the strictness we associate with the German settlers. Typically, in fact, his father once bought a farm and insisted that all nine Wagener children work on it all summer.

As unlikely as it sounds once you've met him, he insists he was the family rebel. "I moved out of the house before I graduated from Guardian Angels High School." Even before then, the love affair began. In his sophomore year, Morrie Wagener bought a 1947 Mercury for the truly shocking sticker price of $100.

"You could see it was special underneath," Morrie says. Almost immediately he got underneath and all over the car. Four years later, he sold it for seven times what he'd paid. ("A $600 profit. Who would've guessed those would end up as the good old days?" Morrie says. Dealers today average less than $400 profit on every new car sold.)

With his siblings off to seminary and college, Morrie the Rebel naturally balked. He decided to attend Dunwoody Institute. That was only partly because of his passion for cars.

"It was partly because I didn't know better. I didn't know about scholarships." So Morrie worked nights and weekends at a gas station to pay his tuition for Dunwoody, which was much lower than a typical college's.

Morrie remembers it as a good school, filled with young men just returning from the Korean War. He learned even more about cars, but remembers something just as lasting. "Dunwoody's mission never was just teaching technical skills.

There also was a huge emphasis on values. Those lessons really took hold." It's a debt Morrie repays every day. He has served on Dunwoody's board of directors since 1995 and regularly leads the fund-raising campaigns that make the nonprofit school a model for technical schools nationwide.

His hard work at Dunwoody—Morrie graduated near the top of the class of 1957—quickly paid off: ten men offered him jobs. Not surprising for a young man who didn't like American cars—"they were bad back then"—Morrie opted to join a small import car dealer on the edge of downtown. Within a year after starting there, opportunity struck in an odd form.

"The owner traveled a lot and the service manager was an alcoholic. By noon each day, he'd pass out. So I took over the service department. There wasn't much choice."

The dysfunctional surroundings, however, made Morrie look for something healthier. In 1958, a salesman at the dealership acquired a franchise in the western suburbs. Morrie signed on. He soon wished he hadn't.

"My first salary check bounced. Turns out this fellow could really work a crowd, but couldn't manage money."

The problems persisted. The owner hired five more techs to work under Morrie—"and their checks bounced, too." But they didn't quit, for a simple reason. Morrie paid them from his own pocket "so they could at least buy groceries and pay rent." This generosity to his employees appears to be a major piece of the puzzle to Morrie's eventual success.

Even more important than these relationships inside, however, were those that Morrie was building outside. He was creating a remarkable business, one client at a time.

That suburban location proved to be another piece. As today, the area was populated by affluent professionals. They particularly appreciated one of Morrie's odd traits. "The owners of the dealership would mark the bills up, and I'd mark them back down." (It's no surprise to learn that today, a handsome framed poster in his showrooms lists as its fifth rule for all the employees: "Always give back.")

Morrie stuck it out and the checks eventually started clearing, although he never was repaid the $2,000 he had spent to cover the unpaid employees. Morrie worked over ninety hours a week and kept his eyes open. Fortunately, his grateful new clients included an industrial psychologist who had become convinced Morrie would make a great owner-dealer. "I'd go out and work on his Triumph convertible, and he'd take a day off to consult with me. This advice and encouragement proved critical."

The big move came in 1966.

Saab was looking to establish a local franchise. Morrie, still partial to foreign cars and to this day a Saab fanatic, wanted in. All he needed was a huge sum: $80,000 for the real estate loan, and another $16,000 for a floor plan loan to finance the cars.

But just as he had made fans among his growing base of customers, word of his devotion and integrity had spread at least as far as the local bank. Without a business plan under his arm, Morrie one afternoon walked into the Northshore Bank in little Wayzata, Minnesota.

Two hours later, he walked out with the loan.

Today, Morrie's empire—twelve dealerships—stretches east to Chippewa Falls and west to Buffalo. It's among the most demanding businesses in the world, a "young person's game," as Morrie describes it: thirteen-hour days, seven-day weeks, and margins so low you'd think they were selling eggs rather than cars. "It's a 2 percent business, basically." There are the interest costs alone: One of Morrie's dealers last month paid $78,000 just in interest.

What keeps him in such a brutal business? It's partly his love of cars, to be sure, and partly the satisfaction that comes not just from building a business, but building relationships—with employees and customers—that endure. "When things are good," he says, "it's the best business in the world." But he adds, "When it's bad, there's nothing harder."

But with a second home in Paradise Valley, Arizona, why don't he and his wife of forty-five years just head off into the sunset, literally? Right now, they're mere visitors there. "Long weekends," he says, "about once a month." No more than that?

"As I said, when the car business is good, there's nothing more fun."

And when it's not?

"There's the fun of coming up with something to make it better."

A morning with Morrie convinces you that this is a unique man. In a modest gray suit and simple black tie, a pair of black Florsheim penny loafers, and the air more of a helpful store clerk than the owner of the entire chain, he appears—well, like that building in the suburbs. You could pass by him without guessing what he has accomplished. You surely could not guess what was inside—a gentleman in the truest sense, perhaps even a throwback to a time of handshake deals and words as bonds. (As evidence, see the statement of values below.)

And after that Tuesday with Morrie, it's easy to begin to think he's right. He really was a rebel.

He still is.

The previous reveals what made Morrie Wagener successful, and how he sold himself. There are several lessons here that defy our usual format of "one story, one moral."

Morrie's not-so-secrets have figured so prominently in his success, and that of his many dealers, that they are posted in the entrance to each of Morrie's dealerships, under the heading "Morrie's Mottos":

Serve. Our fellow Minnesotan Bob Dylan once sang, "You've got to serve somebody." Go beyond that; serve everyone.

Give your all. It satisfies everyone.

Give back. Our parents were right when we tried to hoard cookies from our siblings. They said "share."

Always do right. It works and feels better.

Keep learning. A great education only begins in school; it never ends.

It all starts with love. Love your family, your work, your friends, and our guests, and the blessing of awakening each morning with the chance to really matter.

His success also suggests three more lessons:

Sacrifice. Morrie realized that if you gave a lot, good people would return the favor, and good people are what every business craves. His habit of marking down bills went so far beyond what people had experienced from other dealers that they felt obligated to keep buying their cars from him.

Don't start with the money. Start with something that inspires you so much you will spend all day doing it. Morrie loved cars. He also learned that he also loved giving. The combination carried him beyond his dreams.

Adapt. When Morrie was a teenager, the world's most compact computer weighed twenty-six tons. He was well established in business before computers became a tool, much less productive ones. But he never assumed the old ways were right; he learned new skills, as uncomfortable as the effort made him. And the tools proved indispensable in a business. With such low margins, every savings of productivity can mean the difference between profit and loss.

Be a Morrie.

Arnie

Once again, only Christine can tell this story:

My book *Cancer Has Its Privileges* needed a boost.

Every year, American book publishers unleash 75,000 new books, and potential readers feel overwhelmed by the glut. My effort needed something that would make prospective buyers say, "This looks worth reading."

I knew the perfect person to write the Foreword: Arnold Palmer. He was a household name, he and other members of his family had survived cancer, and I'd known him for almost thirty years.

"Foreword by Arnold Palmer" would prompt thousands of people to pick up my precious baby. I called Arnie's office and spoke to his secretary. She suggested I put my request in writing.

So, I wrote him a letter and enclosed the manuscript, highlighting a golf story so he'd read it first. Within three weeks, I got back his response.

He praised me and my work but wrote, "I am far too busy to write a Foreword that could do justice to your work," and added that he'd never endorsed a product other than his or a corporate sponsor's.

It sounded like no.

I had failed, but only for a split second. I hung up the phone and placed a second call to Florida. It was to Dr. Clarence H. Brown III, aka "Dr. Buck," the CEO of the M. D. Anderson Cancer Center Orlando. We had collaborated on several projects. Better for my purposes, however, I already had given to him without expecting a return. I had donated books to his library, appeared at his annual fund-raiser, and delivered a pro bono presentation as thanks for the presentations for which he had paid me. Not least important, given Dr. Buck's love of golf, I once had sent him two complimentary tickets for my golf tournament.

I asked Dr. Buck if he would write the Foreword. He not only accepted immediately, but asked if there was more he could do to help repay me.

Oh, could he! *Dr. Buck is Arnie's oncologist.*

I told Buck about Arnie's response. Dr. Buck suggested that because Arnie had little time, we could ask him to write an Introduction, which could be just a few sentences, and wouldn't require Arnie to read the entire book. We could rough out a short draft for Arnie, and Buck could take it to him and help Arnie modify it.

Which is just what he did.

I had helped Buck, and Buck wanted to reciprocate. He knew Arnie would respond to the opportunity to reach out himself to cancer patients—if we took the added time to explain it, and saved him time he did not have. By realizing Arnie's only objection was time, and essentially changing our product into something that cost Arnie far less time, we were able to get a valuable endorsement.

Thanks again, Arnie, and you, Dr. Buck.

Yes, giving* does *beget receiving.

Barney

It started with a look in some children's eyes.

Sheryl Leach had seen it in her children's as they watched a video she had made about a dinosaur.

As with most great successes, the genius of Sheryl's video did not spring from her conviction that the world was missing something—in this particular case, good-to-engaging children's television programming. Her faith and that look in her children's eyes was what convinced her. She came to us for help.

She asked our opinion of her video. We said we liked it but pointed out that being well over the ages of five and seven, we didn't fall into the target market. Our children, however, did.

Fortunately, we had learned how to test a children's video. The test isn't whether children watch and appear to enjoy it. It's whether they watch it so many times that they no longer need the sound; they start reciting the dialogue aloud.

Our kids did that.

In the meantime, Sheryl had gotten the video into a test market for Toys "Я" Us. It wasn't moving. The rational observer would conclude there was not a market for the video after all.

Or was there?

The first clue to the marketability of your idea is not the strong interest of many people, but the obvious passion of a significant handful.

Great ideas set off small fires, and they grow.

"I like it." "It's a really nice idea." Those responses are killers. What you want to hear is passion.

Sheryl heard passion, but still her product was

stuck. We launched a contest incentivizing 3,000 field reps to call on anyone—groceries, mass merchandisers, neighborhood gift shops—to carry the video. No after no followed them wherever they called.

Yet Sheryl had heard the passion. She also sensed something else: *we buy with our eyes.*

That makes selling one video difficult. It's just one video, facing spine out on a shelf. A shopper can miss it easily; in fact, a shopper would notice it only if she was actually looking for the video. And even then she might miss it.

Sheryl realized she needed to capture people's eyes. Her simple solution: a cute stuffed dinosaur as a companion to the video. Then, to command more eye and shelf space, two more videos.

We buy with our eyes.

Now she had four products, one of them a vivid visual symbol for the brand. Now she had a branded line rather than a lonely product. Children would see the dinosaur and want one. When they learned their new pet was the star of a movie, they'd want that video, too.

Now Sheryl had people's eyes. Within months she had children's hearts, a television show, clothing line, lunch boxes, paper towels—the empire called Barney.

She persevered, as great salespeople must. But

she persevered because she asked, and listened, and saw and heard the passion.

Are strangers passionate about what you are selling?

If they are, you are there—or just one tweak away. Find the last piece of the puzzle.

If you hear real passion, you are there— or very, very close.

The $18 Million Sandwich

On December 8, 1994, Procter & Gamble handed an until then tiny company an $18 million deal. It was all because of a hamburger, cheese, and pimiento sandwich.

None of the dozens of retail services companies competing for this giant account could have guessed that so much would come down to so little. But all they needed to do was ask.

The story begins in Cincinnati and P&G headquarters. During the previous fall, several executives realized they had created a monster. Over several years they had hired and kept over twenty different firms to help manage their inventory, store stocking, and point of purchase advertising, among other in-store services. With twenty different firms came twenty different invoices, twenty different relationships to manage, and other obvious inefficiencies.

P&G's solution was obvious: consolidate.

The initial tool was obvious, too: an RFP.

With so much money at stake, so much was spent. The competing firms, which ordinarily would send one representative to make their presentations, flew in as many as eight. When weeks after the presentations P&G's committee returned to visit the finalists in their cities, the committee members were feted at several of America's best—and most expensive—restaurants. No wine bill was spared.

But the competitors overlooked something:

Bruce's appetite.

Bruce flew to Minneapolis for a site visit at SPAR Marketing, with a particular desire to ensure that SPAR had the necessary staff and processes to manage such a large account. He arrived at the Minneapolis airport at noon.

He was famished.

Like every other body still standing in the pitch, the SPAR salesperson was eager to impress Bruce and his three P&G colleagues when she greeted them at the airport. She thought a perfect way was to treat them to lunch at The Minikahda Club over-looking Lake Calhoun, or at one of Minneapolis's other close-the-deal restaurants.

Then the woman heard a tiny voice:

"Don't forget to ask."

Instead of deciding to impress the foursome, she decided to do what they would love. What *would* they love? she asked.

Bruce knew. He'd visited the Twin Cities years before and remembered the sandwich of his life-time: hamburger with cheese cooked inside, and pimiento, on a bun. "I don't remember the place, but I'll never forget that sandwich."

"That's the Delwich at the Lincoln Del," the salesperson said. "Right on the way to our office."

Bruce attacked his beloved Delwich with gusto, and the laughter in the Lincoln Del that day gave evidence that the best way to break the ice may be with a sandwich. The group finished and made the short drive to SPAR headquarters. They left, and for SPAR and the competitors, the wait began.

It ended sixteen days later, just after 7:30 A.M.

"I've got good news and bad news for you."
Gulp. Wait, maybe not?

"The good news is, you got our business."

Elation. Wait, maybe not; there's bad news.

And the bad news?

"Same thing: You got *our* business," Bruce laughed, noting P&G's reputation for being a tough client.

How much is the account?

"$18 million." SPAR had doubled, literally, overnight.

What made the difference?

"The sandwich. No one else asked us what we wanted; they assumed we'd be impressed with the fanciest restaurant in their town. We saw dozens of those places. But we only saw one Lincoln Del.

"And I thought anyone who could come up with the right sandwich at the right time would respond to us in other ways, too."

Memorable visuals figure repeatedly in the history of sales. Long after the presentations have ended and the lights have come back up, prospects remember a single visual reminder, and a Vividness Effect takes root. They remember the vivid more clearly, as well as the people associated with it.

Over and again, people choose the vivid.

The Delwich and the noisy Lincoln Del were

vivid, not least because they were unique. Every other competitor for the account opted for a chandeliered restaurant with white linen tablecloths. SPAR opted for the opposite—a noisy delicatessen—and won.

In the end, with twenty companies left standing, someone at Procter & Gamble would say, "Okay, which one was SPAR?" All anyone had to say was, "The Delwich people." Everyone remembered the sandwich, the laughter, and the gesture of simply asking.

As a result, SPAR was the one they remembered—and chose.

Be vivid.

A Day with the World's Greatest Salesperson

Of the world's great feats of salespersonship, none surpasses one that occurred just before 2:00 P.M. on July 16, 2005, in Florence, Italy.

First of all, that time and date are relevant to this feat. Because on that middle-of-summer day, as might be expected, Florence was hot: 93 degrees.

No one on that day would dream of buying a full-length, winter-weight leather coat.

Yet on that day, Raphael Asti sold not just one such coat, but three, and to one couple—a couple who came to Florence looking only for a pair of orange leather shoes.

This feat begins with the very thirsty American couple. They come upon a shaded café on the north edge of a large square, the Piazza Republica. Directly across from them, about the length of a football field away, they spy a replica of the famous Statue of David.

The couple exchange opinions of the sculpture. As the woman finishes, each of them hears a third voice.

"That's not the actual David, you know."

Not wishing to appear rubes (and with the advantage of reading the guidebooks beforehand), the couple turn to the source of the voice, to assure him his news was not news. They see a broad-shouldered, thick-chested thirty-five-year-old man, almost certainly Italian by his skin tone and facial appearance, though not by physique. It appears he could play linebacker for the San Francisco 49ers.

"Oh yes, we know," the Americans proclaim to him, a cappella.

This begins one of those instant, uniquely intense daylong friendships that exist between tourists and the people they encounter. The man introduces himself: Raphael. His command of English immediately becomes obvious: his accent, if anything, hints at Northern California rather than Northern Italy. He explains it. His wife once worked as a buyer for Saks Fifth Avenue, originally from San Francisco.

Interesting! How did they meet? "I called on her," he says. "My family works in leather manufacturing."

They continue to talk. The charming man asks the tourists about honeymoons and the Amalfi Coast of his country; they ask about his wife and children. They learn he has made leather coats for Hillary Clinton and Venus Williams, among other celebrities. (He later confirms this by showing snapshots of the women in his creations.)

Fascinating, they say.

"Would you like to see my coats?" he inquires. "My shop is just a block away."

Absolutely.

He calls his store to alert them that they are coming.

The tourists are greeted warmly at the store,

and immediately spot the source of the young man's pride. While Florence is to leather what Key West is to T-shirts—a place of such over-abundance you would think the law of supply and demand would shrink the prices of leather goods to that of several sticks of gum—they cannot help but see: these are uniquely hand-some pieces.

Raphael quickly finds just the coat for the woman: a fitted chocolate-colored jacket that re-verses to a lighter shade in suede. With her brown hair and olive skin, the woman might actually have inspired this work of art.

It's beautiful. So beautiful, in fact, that they have to ask:

"How much?"

Raphael pulls out a calculator, shows the tag price, then his special price for the couple. By comparison to American stores, his price is irre-sistible, even if the coat would seem to have no earthly function on this scorching day.

Transaction completed—no, not yet.

Raphael asks if they would like to see his main store just yards east of Florence's landmark bridge, the Ponte Vecchio. So close, so yes, of course.

The trio head toward the river.

They are greeted warmly again, this time by a clerk holding a bottle of Chianti wrapped in a red bow. "A gift," she says, and hands it to the surprised couple.

Raphael asks for the couple to see his pièce de résistance. He's right. It is a piece beyond resistance: a full-length fur and leather work in multiple hues of brown. He coaxes his work of art over the woman's shoulders. As if by a miracle, each hue of the coat matches a hue of the woman's hair. She no longer is a mere American tourist. Now, through the miracle of leather and sewing thread, she has become the visiting American movie star.

The couple's next question is inevitable: How much to look like you've been nominated for Best Supporting Actress? Again, Raphael shows the tag price, then the adjusted-just-for-you price. It is the price de résistance.

How can they not pay a fraction of a million dollars to look like that entire sum?

They can't.

Earlier in the fitting, the couple had expressed worry about their lunch reservation. Now that they are done, they learn that the young clerk has booked lunch for them, again with a free bottle of wine "on the store."

But wait, there's more. This remarkable piece, leather with a fox stole around the neck. How flattering, how beautiful—okay, how much? Oh heavens, a fortune in New York at retail and a small fortune in Florence, but with the designer's discount, why, they might as well be at the Gap during inventory clearance! Sold!

The couple arrived in Florence looking only for a pair of orange shoes. They left, on a day too hot for anything heavier than a pair of open-toed sandals, with three coats and a frightening image of their next American Express bill.

What did Raphael do?

He sold by not selling. In fact, from the beginning he seemed to deflect the conversation from his work. Ultimately, he conveyed his pride in his craft, and merely asked if the tourists might like to see it, this being the City of Leather.

He sold with his passion—always a powerful force.

He sold with his empathy. He realized that even his reduced price was more than the couple intended, but he also managed to convey—as so many Italians can, given their view on living each day—that sometimes one must just live.

He created—a key point—a feeling of reciprocity. Raphael offered more than just a bargain price. He included wine, lunch reservations, the "wine-on-us." Each time the couple gave by buying a coat, Raphael gave them something back. Each time that he gave, they felt a need to reciprocate.

Be like Raphael.

Giovanni and the Extraordinary Force of Passion

Kay Redfield Jamison looked around one day, noticed the extraordinary force of a rarely examined emotion, and wrote an enchanting book on the subject.

The subject is *Exuberance*.

You will think of that title if ever you encounter the world's greatest maître d'.

His name is Giovanni Freelli, and his outpost is a cliffside hotel in Ravello, Italy, the celebrated Hotel Caruso.

He's easily noticed. Among other reasons, one notices his resemblance to Robert De Niro in *The Godfather* saga. His formidable Roman nose, forceful chin, olive skin, and slicked-back black hair all trigger that association.

If you are lucky enough to spend several days at his hotel, you notice something else. You saw Giovanni late last night, during the fireworks display from the beach far below. You recall seeing him at lunch, too. Now he is greeting you for breakfast.

You begin to think, although it cannot be true, that he has been there every hour of every day of your visit.

You cannot resist asking.

"Are you working extra hours while they train the second maître d'?" (The hotel has recently re-opened after a several-year renovation, and great maître d's cannot be easy to find in an Italian town so tiny.)

"No."

No? You realize your question was rhetorical; you knew his answer would be Yes. But No?

You mention that you saw him at breakfast, lunch, and dinner, and now at breakfast again. Perhaps there's another explanation: he works three or four days a week, sixteen-hour days, then the second maître d' takes over for the second half of the week. Is that it?

No. He says he works every day but Sunday.

Does he go home each day?

"Yes. For an hour at 4:00 P.M., to shower and change for dinner." (He wears a white coat before 4:00 P.M. and a black coat in the evening.)

"Ninety-six hours a week?" you ask, having multiplied the sixteen hours between eight in the morning until midnight times six days a week.

"Yes."

Heavens! Why?

"This is what I love. I love to be with all of these people, in this place." And unforgettably he adds,

"This is who I am."

One could argue that Giovanni became the world's greatest maître d' simply because of practice. Working twice as many hours a year as the typical person in his profession, he accumulated forty years of experience in his twenty-year career. But no doubt, there is something more.

He has found his passion, and you can feel it. You want to be around him, to be served by him, to feel your sense of life elevated by him.

You know he will do everything he can to make your visit perfect.

And he does.

May you live your passion, too.

THREE THOUGHTS, ONE WISH

We end with three thoughts—no, three passionate convictions.

First, we are struck by the closing stories. They remind us so vividly of the power of giving. Dr. Buck and Arnie gave because someone else had; Morrie Wagener gave for years and still does, and seems truly rich for it; and Raphael received because Raphael gave.

Our book's title seems to suggest to you, "What can I get?" Perhaps if there is only one answer, it's this:

Just give, then watch.

Second, we think of Kurt Vonnegut's book *God Bless You, Mr. Rosewater*, in which Eliot Rosewater's rich uncle advises him on success. Knowing that Eliot lacks all the qualities of an accomplished person, his uncle advises luck:

"Someday a large sum of money will change hands, Eliot," he says. "Get in the middle."

Success is out there. Sometimes you succeed by pursuing it. Other times you succeed simply by being in luck's path when it races by and smacks into you.

Go where you don't want to go. Get in luck's path.

Finally, our title sounds narcissistic. (The late Katharine Hepburn, a famous and admitted narcissist, titled her autobiography *Me*, and we can't resist adding Fred Allen's remark about a narcissist, that "I spotted him walking by holding hands with himself.") The ironic lesson, however, is that we rarely succeed alone; we succeed through others. Others become our customers, friends, mentors, lenders of advice and money. By understanding others, we increase our chances of finding our place.

One day this will make you more money, but every day, it will make you more fulfilled.

You may be like one of the co-authors, an introvert; many readers are. You feel uneasy in this world of relationships, a left-hander in a world of right-handed tools, and following our suggestions comes awkwardly. We understand.

Keep playing. And assume each day there is more you can do to grow, and reap the rewards. We think of the words of a certain poet which we often speak to ourselves in a paraphrase: Live the problems, and do not worry when they persist.

Live the problem, and one day you will live yourself into the solution.

Finally, we think of Henry David Thoreau. Legendarily alone on Walden Pond, communing only with nature and perhaps God, Thoreau encouraged all of us to reach out and seize life.

As E. B. White said of him, Thoreau was beckoning to us all, that "every day is an invitation to its dance."

A remarkable choice of words. Of all the writers in history, none may be harder to picture performing a simple two-step, much less a samba, than Thoreau. But there is his plea, the ultimate message to all of us:

Go to life's dance. Life is a wonder, lived in a blink.

We try to head to the dance whenever we can, and the words in this book have helped us. We hope they help you, too.

Go.

CHRISTINE AND HARRY
March 2007

ABOUT THE AUTHORS

As the strategic director of Beckwith Partners, **HARRY BECKWITH** has led major marketing initiatives for twenty-six Fortune 200 companies, including Wells Fargo, Target, Microsoft, Ernst & Young, and Fidelity Investments.

Harry also is an acclaimed speaker, delivering keynotes to the American Marketing Association, National Speakers Association, and China Fashion Week, lectures at numerous undergraduate and graduate schools of business, and presentations throughout Europe, Asia, and South America.

His first book, *Selling the Invisible* (Warner Books, 1997) was named one of the top ten business and management books of all time and spent thirty-six consecutive months on the *Business Week* best-seller list. Total sales exceed 600,000 copies in seventeen translations. His subsequent books on service marketing and client relationships—*The Invisible Touch* and *What Clients Love*—each became *Business Week* best-sellers, and his reading of *What Clients Love* was a finalist for Audio Book of the Year in 2003.

Harry graduated Phi Beta Kappa from Stanford University. He later served as *Oregon Law Review* Editor-in-Chief, the school's highest honor, and as a law clerk to the Honorable James M. Burns of United States District Court for the District of Oregon.

After seven years in public and private practice, Harry left the law in 1980, and four years later was named creative supervisor of Carmichael Lynch, the fastest promotion in the history of the agency that *Advertising Age* four times has honored as the country's most creative midsized agency.

Harry, who with his wife, Christine Clifford Beckwith, is the father of six children, also is a Masters bridge player and avid athlete. Since 1975 he has run over 55,000 miles—more than one and a half times around the world.

CHRISTINE CLIFFORD BECKWITH is the sales director of Beckwith Partners, and CEO/President of The Cancer Club, today the world's largest producer of humorous and helpful products for people with cancer.

As Senior Executive Vice President for SPAR Marketing Services, and the top salesperson in the retail services industry for over eight years, Christine was responsible for accounts with Kmart, Toys 'Я Us, Procter & Gamble, AT&T, Mattel Toys, and Revlon.

Diagnosed with breast cancer in 1994, Christine went on to write four award-winning portrayals of her story in her books entitled *Not Now . . . I'm Having a No Hair Day* (University of Minnesota Press, 1996), *Our Family Has Cancer, Too!* (written especially for children, University of Minnesota Press, 1998), *Cancer Has Its Privileges: Stories of Hope and Laughter* (Penguin Putnam, 2003), and *Your Guardian Angel's Gift* (Bronze Bow Publishing, 2005).

Christine attended the University of Denver and University of Minnesota majoring in speech communication. She was awarded the Order of the Delta Gamma Rose from the sorority for her distinguished contributions to the world and for her national recognition.

Host of the Christine Clifford Celebrity Golf Invitational, a benefit for breast cancer research, Christine has raised over $1.25 million for the cause. She has been awarded "The Council of Excellence Award" for income development from the American Cancer Society.

Christine has received her CSP designation (Certified Speaking Professional) from the National Speakers Association, a recognition accorded to the top 7 percent of professional speakers worldwide.

Christine and Harry live in Minneapolis, Minnesota, with their semi-legendary flying cat, Simone, and whichever of their many children might be visiting.

For information about their consulting, teaching, and speaking services on positioning, branding, and client relationships, visit Beckwithpartners.com or call Beckwith Partners at 612-305-4420. E-mail Harry at: invisble@bitstream.net (please note the missing letter "i") to subscribe to his newsletter.

For information about Christine and The Cancer Club, visit cancerclub.com, ChristineClifford.com, or call 952-944-0639. E-mail Christine at:

Christine@cancerclub.com.